IMAGES
of America

OLD FORT JACKSON

On the Cover: Volunteer reenactors like these 1970s Revolutionary War ones on the parade ground bring Fort Jackson to life. From right to left, the men portray a free black soldier in the French Volunteers du Saint Domingue from Haiti, a fusilier (regular soldier) from the French Regiment du Foix, and three 2nd South Carolina Continentals, who were professional American soldiers. While Fort Jackson was built beginning in 1808, an earlier Revolutionary War "mud fort" was constructed on the site, too. The regiments represented here fought in the 1779 Battle of Savannah. That battlefield is located in today's downtown Savannah. Lt. Col. Francis "Swamp Fox" Marion led the 2nd South Carolina Continentals when they assaulted the Spring Hill Redoubt with their French allies. The Haitian volunteers helped stave off the British while the Americans and their allies retreated. (Courtesy of Coastal Heritage Society.)

IMAGES
of America

OLD FORT JACKSON

Laura Seifert

ARCADIA
PUBLISHING

ISBN 978-1-4671-0612-2

Published by Arcadia Publishing
Charleston, South Carolina

Printed in the United States of America

Library of Congress Control Number: 2020943660

For all general information, please contact Arcadia Publishing:
Telephone 843-853-2070
Fax 843-853-0044
E-mail sales@arcadiapublishing.com
For customer service and orders:
Toll-Free 1-888-313-2665

Visit us on the Internet at www.arcadiapublishing.com

For John Roberson (1960–2017), artificer extraordinaire

Contents

Acknowledgments

Thanks to Scott Smith, Jeff Reed, Greg Starbuck, Dr. William Kelso, Talley Kirkland, Jeff Kirkland, Beth Reiter, Kelly Zacovic, Dr. Ervan Garrison, Kyle Griffith, Michael Jordan, Sarah Jones, Tanya Milton, Kurt Knoerl, Tania Sammons, and Libby Fay for answering my questions. Justin Childers and Aaron Bradford carefully analyzed the soldiers' cartes de visite and graciously answered my stream of questions. John Roberson, we thank you for your life's work and dedication to the fort, years of care, and diligence in maintaining and curating both museum objects and things we never knew we needed. Thanks for your amazing breadth of knowledge and humor, which is still making us laugh as we continually discover your legacy. This book would never have been possible without Lydia Moreton. She is truly my coconspirator and partner on this project.

Unless otherwise noted, all images appear courtesy of the Coastal Heritage Society.

INTRODUCTION

Staff at Old Fort Jackson like to proclaim that the fort has never been taken by the enemy. The truth is, Fort Jackson has rarely seen an enemy. Georgia's oldest brick fort has sat through many wars but has only been under fire twice in over 200 years. Despite this, Fort James Jackson, named for the Georgia governor and United States senator, has plenty of drama and human stories.

Fort Jackson is one of five remaining Second System fortifications in the United States. The others are Fort Columbus and Castle Williams in New York, Castle Pinckney in South Carolina, and Fort Norfolk, Virginia. Fort Jackson is unique among these survivors as it retains most of its original fabric, design, and function, even though later additions were made. The 26 original Second System fortifications were constructed between 1807 and 1814, most with brick rather than earth, and many were under the direction of recent West Point graduates. Fort Jackson is typical of these coastal fortifications, which had five elements: a battery, a palisade, barracks, magazines, and a hot shot furnace for heating ordnance before firing.

Nichol Turnbull sold Wharf Lot No. 12, a 2.3-acre lot, to the US government for $1,800 in 1808. This riverfront property was across from Five Fathom Hole, a 30-foot-deep, strategic site in the Savannah River. Here, ships unloaded their cargo onto barges or waited for high tide to sail into Savannah's wharves themselves. Capt. William McRee, US Army Corps of Engineers and a recent West Point graduate, directed construction of the brick masonry battery starting in late 1808. Slow progress was made until 1810 when the project ran out of money. Fear of yellow fever and malaria often halted work during the summer months. The impending War of 1812 jump-started construction again in March 1812. The fort itself was mostly finished by the summer, when it was staffed with local militia like the Chatham Artillery and the Republican Blues as well as parts of the 8th Regiment, US Army Infantry. Building magazines and constructing the landward wooden palisade continued into 1813. Troops stayed until 1815, although the fort saw no action during the War of 1812.

The battery's earliest iteration was a 10- to 11-foot-high, arc-shaped wall of brick. The earthen parapet, or gun platform, tucked behind it was 17 to 18 feet deep, 21 feet above high water, and 78 yards long. Underneath the gun platform were three wooden barracks and two arched magazines. Behind the western end of the battery was a hot shot furnace with a 50- to 60-ball capacity. Hot shot furnaces were used to heat cannon balls to extreme temperatures before firing, so when the heated ball hit a wooden ship, it would set it on fire. The whole structure was supported by cypress timbers driven into the gray clay. The palisade enclosing the fort landward was constructed of square timbers and ran 100 yards long and 9 feet high. The original moat was simply a low ditch that was filled by the rising tide.

By 1821, the fort was inconsistently staffed and already deteriorating. Company H, 4th US Heavy Artillery sometimes garrisoned the fort, but yellow fever remained a serious problem. Between 1823 and 1844, Fort Jackson only received occasional repairs from the Army Corps of Engineers. Also during this period, the US Health Officer used Five Fathom Hole to quarantine boats until

1827. A fire on April 14, 1833, burned down the wooden buildings, including the quarters and gun platform. Newspaper reports suggested arson, but Lieutenant Mansfield, the Army Corps officer who surveyed the fort, assumed careless fishermen squatting in the barracks were the source. The magazine, while untouched by fire, had rotten doors and floors, and thieves had stolen the door hinges. The fort's hot shot furnace was ironically unscathed by the fire.

The situation changed in 1845 when impending war with Mexico prompted Congress to authorize funding to repair and ready Fort Jackson for war. Despite the larger, flashier Fort Pulaski, built between 1829 and 1847, Fort Jackson was a key asset. Ships could still attack Savannah by sailing through Warsaw Sound and up the Wilmington River, avoiding Fort Pulaski altogether.

US Army Corps lieutenant B.S. Alexander was in charge of major renovations. The wood casemates were replaced with 18 arched masonry casemates while the two original magazines were repaired. A new magazine was built at the southwest end of the casemates. The battery was raised three feet, and the wooden palisade was replaced with a 20-foot brick wall and four demi-bastions. The wall is three feet thick with loopholes (tall, very thin windows). A drawbridge was added to the sally port, and a stone stairway now gave easier access to the parapet. Renovations continued in spurts through the late 1840s and into the 1850s. Work proceeded mostly in the cooler months, avoiding the hot summer with its risks of heat exhaustion and mosquito-borne diseases. By 1857, a wet moat ditch, 20 feet wide and 7 feet deep, was built. The ditch had wood flooring and a counterscarp retaining wall that encircled the fort, coming together at the river side with a brick and concrete tide tunnel and gate. This arched tunnel allowed river water to flow into and out of the moat with the tides. The tide tunnel doubled as a dock, replacing the old wooden wharf. Two brick enlisted men's barracks were built, and the foundation was laid for an officers' barracks, but it was never completed. While there were extensive additions in this period, the original fabric remained intact; the new was added on rather than replacing the old.

On January 26, 1861, Georgia state militia took over Fort Jackson and declared it Confederate property. Many Confederate units were attached to the fort during the Civil War, including the 4th Louisiana, 1st Georgia Volunteers, and the 1st Georgia Regiment. Even early in the war, conditions at the fort could be uncomfortable. Heat, mosquitoes, and poor diet plagued the soldiers. A letter from "Dixie" on May 16, 1861, to the editor in the *Savannah Daily Morning News* remonstrated the soldiers' treatment and specifically the lack of vegetables: "Why is it that the troops at Fort Jackson have not had any favors extended to them? . . . They are in the midst of the rice fields, where mosquitoes are as thick as rice and as large as humming birds."

Robert E. Lee, tasked with improving the Savannah River defenses, visited the fort several times in 1862. Lee evacuated the barrier islands, whose widely spread defenses were unsustainable. This action gave the Union troops an advantage when they took Fort Pulaski on April 11, 1862, and left Fort Jackson as the last major barrier between the Union army and Savannah. On October 1, 1862, Fort Jackson saw its only serious engagement. Two Union steamers, the *Planter* and *Starlight*, took on Confederate steamboats, which retreated under fire to Fort Jackson. The *Planter* fired at Fort Jackson with its 30-pounder Parrot rifle. Fort Jackson could not return fire because the ships were too far away, and their inferior smooth bore cannons could not fire as far. Fort Bartow at Causton's Bluff attempted to fire on the Union steamers, but the *Planter*'s fire stopped them. Newspapers reported that 100 shots were fired at the fort in about an hour, but there was no damage to the fort.

Confederate general William Hardee ordered the evacuation of Savannah and the river batteries on December 20, 1864, and 12,000 troops made their way to South Carolina that night. At Fort Jackson, Confederate troops burned the barracks, spiked the guns, and shoved ammunition into the moat. Her sailors sunk the CSS *Georgia*. The following day, Union troops occupied Fort Jackson, including the 28th Regiment Pennsylvania Veteran Volunteers Infantry and the 29th Regiment Ohio Volunteer Infantry. When federal troops raised the US flag, the CSS *Savannah*, a Confederate ironclad, shot at the fort. This was the second time, albeit minor, that the fort came under fire. The CSS *Savannah* continued upriver and was intentionally sunk before she could be captured. On April 11, 1865, Savannah got news of the fall of Richmond and the war's end. Each river battery saluted in turn, starting with the Union warship *Pontiac* then Fort Jackson. This is believed to be the last time a Fort Jackson cannon was fired (excepting modern demonstrations).

After the Civil War, Fort Jackson operated very briefly as a port quarantine station in 1867. In 1869, the Board of Engineers reviewed coastal forts because rifling technology made Second and Third System forts woefully outdated. Some modifications were made to Fort Jackson in the early 1870s, such as building the c. 1873 shell magazine and installing several new guns; however, renovations were extremely expensive, and little of the larger plan was completed. The Army Corps of Engineers shifted to minimal upkeep, and without regular maintenance, the guns quickly became unserviceable.

A June 1883 condition report showed the gun platform, which had been adapted for new guns, was so rotted that "not one gun could be safely fired." The guns and iron carriages were in "fair condition." The next year, the fort's name changed to Fort Oglethorpe to avoid confusion with other Fort Jacksons, including one in South Carolina, which is still an active military base today. The fort had a series of caretakers and $480 per year for maintenance. Daniel Z. Duncan, an African American Union army veteran, was one of these keepers from 1889 to 1908, when he transferred to Jones Island. He spent 45 years in government service before he retired in 1914 at the age of 72.

In preparation for the Spanish-American War, Fort Jackson's guns were removed in April 1898. During this process, two fell into the moat and had to be salvaged with barges. The guns were sent to Brunswick, Georgia. In 1905, the name reverted to Fort Jackson, to avoid confusion with Fort Oglethorpe in north Georgia. Eventually, the City of Savannah bought the property in 1923 with the aim of creating a park. The Great Depression and World War II intervened, and in the 1940s, Southeastern Shipyards bought the property and other surrounding land. Their factory made Liberty ships and minesweepers for the war effort. Next, the American Cyanamid Company purchased the land in 1955. After several attempts to give away the fort to a preservation-minded buyer, the State of Georgia finally bought the fort in 1965 for $1. The Georgia Historical Commission operated the Fort Jackson Maritime Museum between 1969 and 1975, but the site closed with budget cuts. Coastal Heritage Society, a brand new nonprofit, leased Old Fort Jackson and reopened to the public on Labor Day 1976, exactly one year after the site was shuttered. Coastal Heritage Society still manages the fort today.

This artist's rendition shows the fort in its earliest iteration as a Second System fortification. The fort looks significantly different, with a wood palisade and simple wooden door rather than an imposing brick wall and drawbridge. The moat is a tidal ditch, rather than a formal, brick-walled moat, which would not be built until the late 1850s.

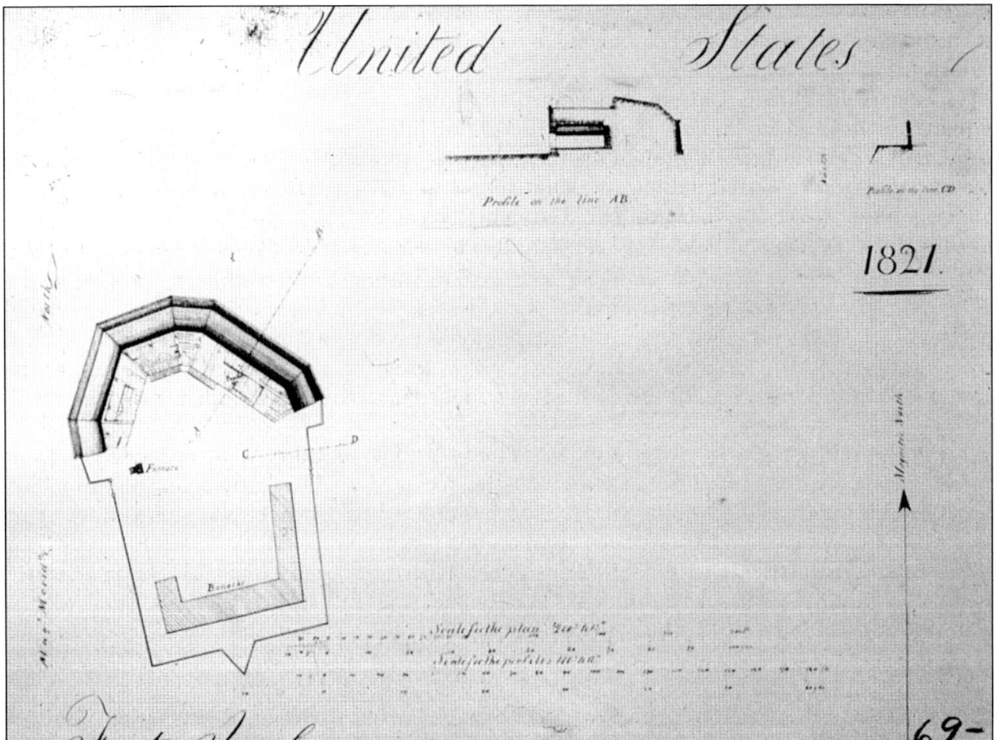

When this 1821 map was drawn, the fort was already deteriorating and staffed intermittently. This map shows Fort Jackson still in its earliest configuration with a brick battery facing the river and a wood palisade protecting the rear, landward side. Within the fort were three wooden barracks and a magazine under the gun platform. The hot shot furnace is on the west side behind the battery.

One

From Mud to Brick

Building the Fort and Its Early History

Thomas Salter, the first colonial owner of this property, operated a brickyard on the "island," which was really an area of higher elevation in the marsh. Four people produced about 11,000 bricks per day with the gray clay. Salter later moved to Hutchinson Island for better clay resources but died of fever in 1751. In September 1777, the Georgia Executive Council designated $3,000 to build a mud fort on Salter's Island across from Five Fathom Hole, a strategic location as the river's last deep section before Savannah. Capt. Thomas Lee and his garrison were sent to build the fort. Very little is known about this Revolutionary War–era "mud fort," but it was likely a basic earthen battery. Unfortunately, Lee got yellow fever (or malaria by some sources) at the fort and died in February 1778. The fort was abandoned, and the British sailed upriver and took Savannah later that year.

In the early 1800s, rice fields surrounded Salter's Island when Capt. William McRee was sent to supervise construction on Fort Jackson. McRee received his US Army commission in 1805 upon graduating from West Point. In 1808, he was only 20 years old, but he had spent the past two years surveying along the southern coast and had some experience.

Newspaper advertisements give little insights to these very early years. One advertised for painters to paint the barracks as follows: "The top red, sides yellow, windows shutter and doors, red." After the War of 1812, the fort was garrisoned intermittently, and desertions were not uncommon. An 1817 newspaper listed three soldiers (all privates) who deserted from Fort Jackson. The advertisement offered $20 to anyone who returned two of the deserters. Pvt. Isham Still, the third deserter, was described as having a "dark complexion, black eyes, dark hair." The Army only offered $10 for Still's return, all suggesting Still was a free person of color.

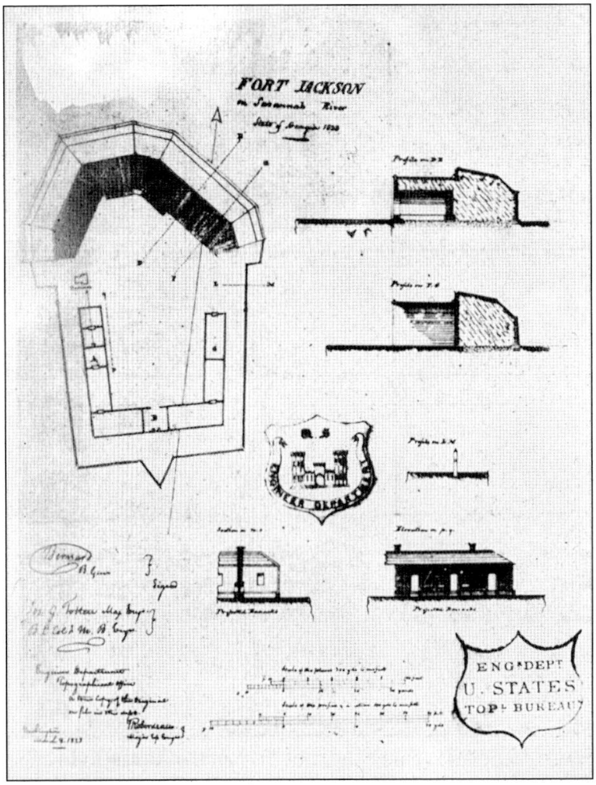

Between 1815 and 1844, the fort was largely abandoned, with the Army Corps of Engineers only doing essential repairs to maintain the structure, especially while focused on building Fort Pulaski. The report accompanying this 1823 map noted that the platform and ramp were rotten and the barracks were falling down, but the rest was well preserved.

The fort is largely made of Savannah grey bricks. The center brick pictured here has finger imprints from the enslaved person who pressed the clay into a mold. The dried, molded clay was then kiln fired to create a brick. Enslaved persons handmade most Savannah grey bricks on Henry McAlpin's Hermitage Plantation, a few miles from Savannah along the Savannah River.

Built in the late 1850s in Charleston, South Carolina, this Smith & Porter steam engine is the same type that was used at Fort Jackson during the pre–Civil War renovations. This state-of-the-art technology was used to pump water from the moat, drive pilings, and do other heavy labor. Its advantages included that it did not get tired or contract yellow fever. This steam engine came to Fort Jackson in 1979, and staff and volunteers restored it on-site. In these pictures, the newly restored engine is shuttled to its new location in the fort. It is the oldest steam engine still in existence.

John Roberson led the team that renovated the Smith & Porter steam engine. Here, he is manufacturing new metal parts to replace ones that were either missing or too damaged to be rehabilitated and reused. Roberson's expertise can be seen throughout the fort and other Coastal Heritage Society properties. He was an interpreter, blacksmith, carpenter, exhibit fabricator, backhoe operator, black powder certified handler, a font of historical knowledge, and much more. The funding for the steam engine restoration came from local donations as well as an Institute of Museum and Library Services grant for $13,550. Once completed, the steam engine made its debut entrance and unveiling at the ever popular Coastal Heritage Society (CHS) annual membership oyster roast. The steam engine currently resides at another CHS–managed site, the Georgia State Railroad Museum, and is displayed in the Tender Frame Shop.

Two

The Men of Fort Jackson

The Soldiers Who Did Not Fight Here

Soldiers at Fort Jackson faced many challenges. It was very cold in the winter. Especially later in the Civil War, soldiers were often poorly supplied and went without enough winter coats and blankets. It was very hot in the summer. Mosquitoes carrying malaria and yellow fever were a real threat, if still unrecognized as the connection between mosquitoes and disease was not understood. In fact, the mosquitoes killed far more combatants than enemy soldiers. In addition, the stress of anticipating attacks and constantly being on guard was exhausting.

Very little is known about the first men who served at Fort Jackson. During the War of 1812, local militias like the Republican Blues, Chatham Artillery, and Savannah Artillery garrisoned the fort with the 8th Regiment, United States Infantry and the 2nd United States Artillery. The 4th Regiment of Artillery was officially posted there in the early 1820s, but it is unclear how much time they actually spent at the fort. Often in summer, troops were cycled between Savannah and Fort Jackson, reducing exposure to mosquito-borne diseases.

Later years are better documented through the Army's records and civilian accounts. It is known that the 1st Georgia Regulars and the 22nd Georgia Heavy Artillery, which included the Bartow Artillery (Company A), Montgomery Guards (Company E), and the Emmett Rifles (Company F), served at Fort Jackson during the Civil War. Other Confederate military units included the Oglethorpe Light Artillery, Irish Jasper Greens, Republican Blues (Infantry), 4th Louisiana Infantry, and Company K (Mercer Artillery) of the 28th Battalion Georgia Siege Artillery. The Union troops included the 137th New York Infantry Regiment, 29th Ohio Infantry Regiment, and the 28th Pennsylvania Infantry Regiment, all from John Geary's 2nd "White Star" Division. The 55th Massachusetts Infantry Regiment, an African American unit formed once the famous 54th Massachusetts was full, took over for the 2nd Division regiments and served at Forts Jackson, Bartow, and Battery Lee until February 1, 1865.

The fort is named after James Jackson, a soldier and politician who served Georgia for nearly 30 years. In 1772, a 15-year-old James Jackson arrived in Savannah from Devonshire, England, to study law. He spent few years as a lawyer, however, because he joined the Georgia militia to fight for the American Revolution, serving six years. After independence, he married Mary Charlotte Young in 1785 and had six children. Jackson joined the Georgia legislature and served in the first United States Congress and later the US Senate, where he became embroiled in the Yazoo scandal. In 1798, he was elected governor of Georgia, and he finished his career back in the US Senate from 1801 to 1806, when he died in office at the age of 48. Known for his temper, Jackson participated in several duels and fistfights.

Sgt. Richard Millen Jr. enlisted in the 18th Battalion of the Georgia Infantry, also known as the Savannah Volunteer Guards (SVG). The 18th Battalion was not stationed at Fort Jackson; they were approximately two miles east at Fort Boggs for a good portion of the war before leaving for the Charleston area and later Virginia. This picture was taken early in the war, based on the uniform, which includes a Georgia state seal on his belt buckle and an SVG on his cap. The uniform frock coat is likely jean wool, a cotton/wool mix that was usually light brown or possibly light blue. He carries a smooth-bore Springfield musket, model 1842, and wears a knapsack. Millen died on April 6, 1865. He was killed in the Battle of Sayler's Creek in Virginia, along with 82 percent of his unit, two days before the Confederacy surrendered. Millen's parents brought him back from Virginia and reburied him in Laurel Grove Cemetery, where he lies with the rest of his family.

OUR VISITORS, THE REPUBLICAN BLUES OF SAVANNAH, GEORGIA.—PHOTOGRAPHED BY BRADY.—[SEE NEXT PAGE.]

Republican Blues were some of the first soldiers to garrison the fort during the War of 1812, but this *Harper's Weekly* image dates just prior to the Civil War, August 4, 1860. The Republican Blues, along with the Irish Jasper Greens, were some of the local Savannah militias who garrisoned the fort in 1861 under the command of Capt. J.W. Anderson. Shortly after Georgia seceded in March 1861, excursion boats took civilians to tour the forts and batteries along the Savannah River. A party atmosphere prevailed until the summer months, when the mosquitoes arrived. These militia troops were not highly trained. Captain Anderson's brother Edward sailed up the Savannah River in November 1861 on the blockade runner *Fingal*. Edward Anderson noted in his diary, "I smiled as I looked at the guns on the parapet. They were mounted on two logs placed parallel with each other, with the trunnions [*sic*] of the cannon supported upon them. They could never have been fired without jumping off into the area of the fort."

Dougald Ferguson (1838–1892) dressed in his Republican Blues officer's dress uniform for this portrait. He joined the Republican Blues at the age of 19 in 1857 and entered the Confederate army in their ranks, mustering in at Fort Jackson under Captain Anderson as a corporal. After two years, he joined the 5th Georgia Cavalry, serving until the war's end. Ferguson married Ann Margaret, and they had four children together. In 1865, he entered into a business partnership with Capt. W.D. Dixon, forming Ferguson & Dixon Undertaker's Wareroom. After 10 years, each man began a solo business. Considered a leading undertaker, Ferguson continued until paralysis from a stroke forced him to quit working for the last few years of his life. Approximately 40 members of the Republican Blues attended his funeral, firing three volleys over his grave and playing "Taps." He is buried in Laurel Grove North Cemetery. Captain Dixon was his funeral director.

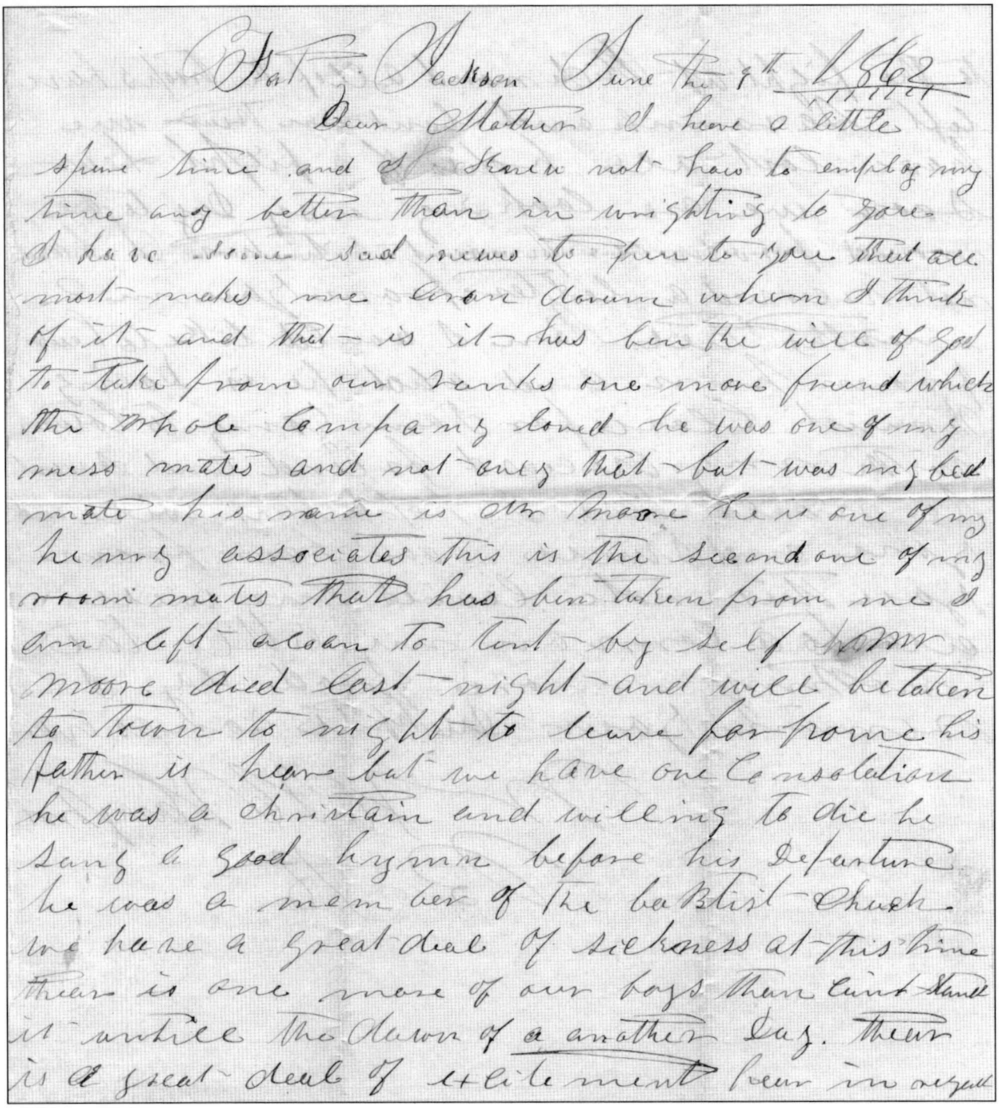

Fort Jackson June the 9th 1862
Dear Mother I have a little
spare time and I know not how to employ my
time any better than in wrighting to you.
I have some sad news to pen to you that all
most makes me cry down when I think
of it and that is it has ben the will of God
to take from our ranks one more friend which
the whole Company loved he was one of my
mess mates and not only that but was my bed
mate his name is Mr Moore he is one of my
henry associates this is the second one of my
room mates that has ben taken from me I
am left aloan to tent by self Mr
Moore died last night and will be taken
to town to night to leave for home his
father is hear but we have one Consolation
he was a christain and willing to die he
sang a good hymn before his departure
he was a mem ber of the baptist Church.
we have a great deal of sickness at this time
there is one more of our boys than cant stand
it untill the dawn of a another day. theur
is a great deal of excitement hear in regard

W.H.H. Vaughan frequently wrote letters to his mother while serving in the Confederate army. The Coastal Heritage Society has 17 of these letters written from various stations in Georgia including Fort Bartow, Camp Skidaway, St. John's Hospital in Savannah, Camp "Deptferd" [*sic*], Camp Chapman in Griffin, and Fort Jackson. He frequently complained that his mother did not respond to his letters, and wrote that while he promised to write every week, it was not always possible. He often included details about his station and enemy locations, once casually mentioning his court-martial. In this letter, written from Fort Jackson on June 9, 1862, and in other letters, he relates the loss of friends and fellow soldiers. Health details and deaths were frequent themes. He had measles in November 1861, but in this letter, he is well except for "a corn on my little toe."

Georgia native Gen. William Joseph Hardee (1815–1873) was nicknamed "Old Reliable" for his excellence in military tactics and his talent in training soldiers. His 1855 textbook *Rifle and Light Infantry Tactics* was required reading on both sides of the Civil War. When that war began, he resigned from the US Army and joined the Confederate army as a colonel. Rapidly promoted to major general, he fought in Kentucky and Tennessee before the Atlanta Campaign. General Hardee used his tactics most effectively to evacuate the greatly outnumbered Confederate troops from Savannah as Union general Sherman advanced. Hardee arrived only days before Sherman and refused to surrender in order to give his troops time to evacuate. The night of December 20, 1864, Confederate troops assembled either at River Street for evacuation via pontoon bridge or at Fort Jackson. Troops leaving Fort Jackson destroyed everything of military value, including burning the interior buildings, before taking a steamship to South Carolina.

The following four photographs are cartes de visite of enlisted men who served in Company E, 28th Regiment, Pennsylvania Infantry. Company E was recruited from Carbon County. The white star on their uniforms indicates they served in the Second Division of the 12th Army Corps, under the command of John White Geary, which included the 28th Pennsylvania and 29th Ohio. These two regiments were the first to raise the Union flag at Fort Jackson on December 21, 1864. William Weiss, pictured here, enlisted on July 6, 1861, as a private and mustered into Company E, 28th Pennsylvania, which was organized in Philadelphia. Weiss was possibly promoted to corporal, as indicated by the two service chevrons on his sleeves. He was wounded on June 24, 1864, at Marietta, Georgia, and he died of his wounds on July 10, 1864. He is buried at Chattanooga, Tennessee.

Like Weiss, Cpl. Aaron Moser wears a nine-button frock coat. A light blue vest and trousers complete his uniform. On September 3, 1861, Moser enlisted as a 24-year-old private. He was promoted to sergeant. Moser died in early May 1864 of his wounds received at the Battle of Mill Creek Gap, Georgia.

William Johnson enlisted on July 6, 1861, as a private. He mustered out on July 18, 1865, at Washington, DC. Johnson wears a less formal, nine-button shell jacket. His pants and vest are light blue, and the buttons on his vest and coat as well as his chevrons are tinted gold in the original photograph. The background curtain is tinted purple.

William Smith is dressed similarly to his fellow soldiers, except for his civilian vest, cravat, and pocket watch. Little is known about this man. Two William Smiths enlisted in Company E (one deserted, the other mustered out at war's end). At least five more William Smiths enlisted in the 28th Pennsylvania. This photograph was taken in Allentown, suggesting this man served in Company E.

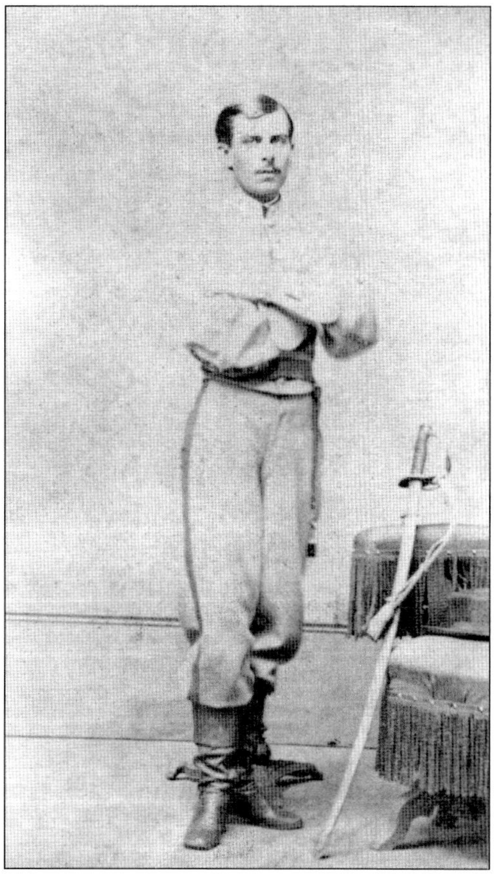

"Looking at this I think of the original and remember him in your prayers" is written on the back of this photograph. This unidentified man is likely a cavalryman, given his boots and sword. He is wearing a shell jacket, and his trousers likely had dashing red stripes. His uniform appears to be from earlier, rather than later, in the war.

At age 24, shoemaker William Nutt enlisted in Company I, Massachusetts 2nd Infantry Regiment on May 25, 1861. He was quickly promoted to lieutenant and commissioned an officer in Company F, Massachusetts 54th Infantry Regiment in April 1863. This is the African American regiment made famous in the movie *Glory*. A few months later, he was transferred to Company D, Massachusetts 55th Infantry Regiment and promoted to full captain. From January 13 to February 1, 1865, the 55th Regiment's Companies C, D, and F were on duty at Fort Jackson. Other companies were stationed at neighboring Battery Lee and Fort Bartow. The regiment was tasked with cleaning up the fort and remounting the cannons after the Confederates' abrupt and disruptive departure. Nutt mustered out of the Union army on August 29, 1865, in Charleston, South Carolina, as a full lieutenant colonel. He died in August 1909 in his hometown of Natick, Massachusetts.

Some soldiers left their mark on the fort quite literally. Many of the soft Savannah grey bricks bear the initials or other identifying information of past inhabitants and visitors. Some of this graffiti is quite old, while some is much more modern. R.F. Hunt, who served in Company D, 4th Virginia Regiment, graffitied on the main magazine's south wall.

A second graffiti mark reads, "JJD C D 4Va P L," and more initials are scratched in below by other soldiers from Company D, 4th Virginia. This regiment passed through Savannah in 1898 when traveling to Cuba to fight in the Spanish-American War. While in Savannah, they stopped at Fort Jackson to do some sightseeing

Three

The Civil War

Fort Jackson Anchors the Network

In January 1861, Georgia officials demanded the keys to Fort Jackson and Fort Pulaski, both of which had no permanent garrison at the time. A "fort keeper" was maintaining Fort Jackson. Federal officials complied. Local and state militia were manning the fort by the end of the month, including the Republican Blues and the Irish Jasper Greens, under the command of Capt. J.W. Anderson.

One year after the Confederates fired on Fort Sumter, beginning the war, the Union army captured Fort Pulaski, located on Cockspur Island, about 10 miles downriver from Fort Jackson. This left Fort Jackson as the primary barrier between the Union forces and Savannah. The Union did not continue moving in from the east, however, for two reasons. One, there was a major yellow fever outbreak, leaving both sides depleted. And second, the CSS *Georgia* was already in place, although work was still being completed into the early summer of 1862.

While Fort Jackson could be considered the anchor, it was only one part of the larger system of defenses surrounding Savannah. For example, Fort Bartow, the Causton's Bluff battery, lay less than a mile and a half south on St. Augustine Creek, while Fort Boggs was two miles to the southwest at Brewton Hill. The ironclad CSS *Georgia* was anchored in the Savannah River across and slightly upstream from Fort Jackson, acting as a floating battery. Numerous river obstructions such as wooden cribs and spiles, or large wood stakes, also blocked ships from coming upriver. Battery Lee was directly east of the fort, nearly within shouting distance.

This newspaper illustration shows the southeast corner of Fort Jackson, including the wooden barracks and brick chimneys within, and Battery Lee to the east (right side). In early 1862, Gen. Robert E. Lee inspected the area forts and ordered an earth battery built about 200 yards downstream from Fort Jackson. Battery Lee was originally called Alligator Battery because it sat

so low next to the water. Visible between the fortifications is the railroad line, which brought much needed supplies to the men. In the far distance are likely Union ships, part of the blockade that formed from 1862 until the war's end.

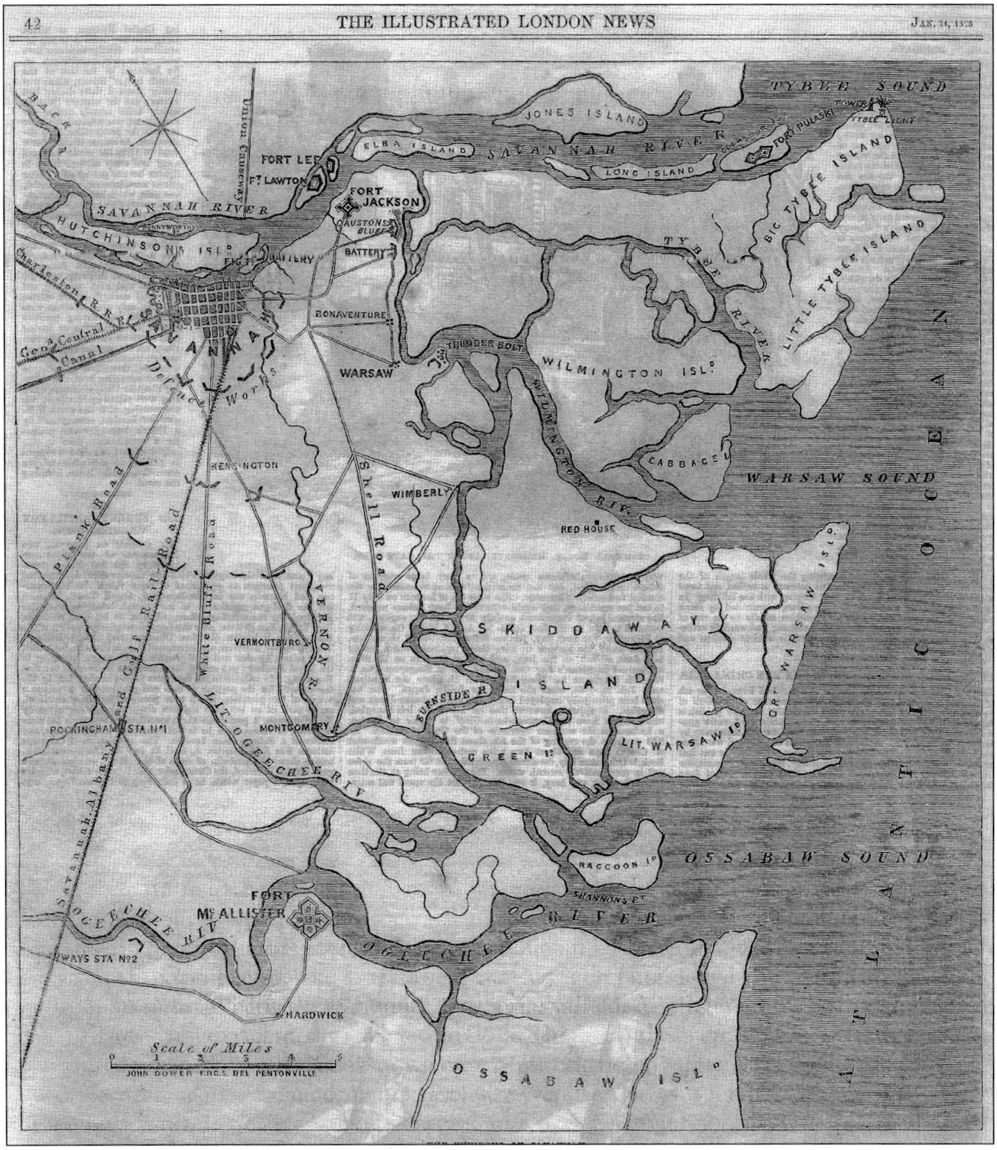

This map of Savannah's defense network was published in the *Illustrated London News* on January 14, 1865. The map is largely accurate, but there are some errors. For example, Battery Lee (also known as Fort Lee) is on the wrong side of the river. This map is also greatly simplified, and many small batteries are missing, such as Fort Boggs, which was just west of Fort Jackson. The map also shows multiple railroad lines, which were critical for supplying the Army. At the southern end of the map is Fort McAllister, an earthen fort on the Ogeechee River. Today, Fort McAllister is a state park. Note the "Red House" on Skidaway Island. The Bartow Artillery was stationed near here in 1862 and left when General Lee ordered the islands evacuated. They were later assigned to Fort Jackson. The Red House property later became a monastery and freedmen's school.

INTERIOR OF FORT JACKSON

In February 1862, Gen. Robert E. Lee assigned Maj. Edward Anderson to take command of Fort Jackson and Battery Lee and strengthen the defenses. Anderson was a highly respected retired naval officer who had previously noted the dire straits of Fort Jackson's gun platform in his diary. His improvements included adding traverses between heavy guns on the parapet, building a covered walkway or earthen bank along the fort's east wall, and leaning railroad iron against the magazine and over the fort's entrances. In this illustration, the traverses, or earthen mounds between the cannons, can be seen on the gun platform, and the railroad iron can be seen at the end of the barracks on the left. Also of note is the fountain at the center, which was located over a natural spring. (Courtesy of the City of Savannah Municipal Archives.)

FORT JACKSON, LOOKING WEST.

The rice fields surrounding Fort Jackson can be seen in the foreground. Rice plantations were a major economic driver in Georgia from the mid-18th century into the later 19th century. Rice plantations were brutally labor intensive. Enslaved people performed the vast majority of this labor, both the physical work as well as the planning and cultivation skills originally brought from Africa. (Courtesy of the City of Savannah Municipal Archives.)

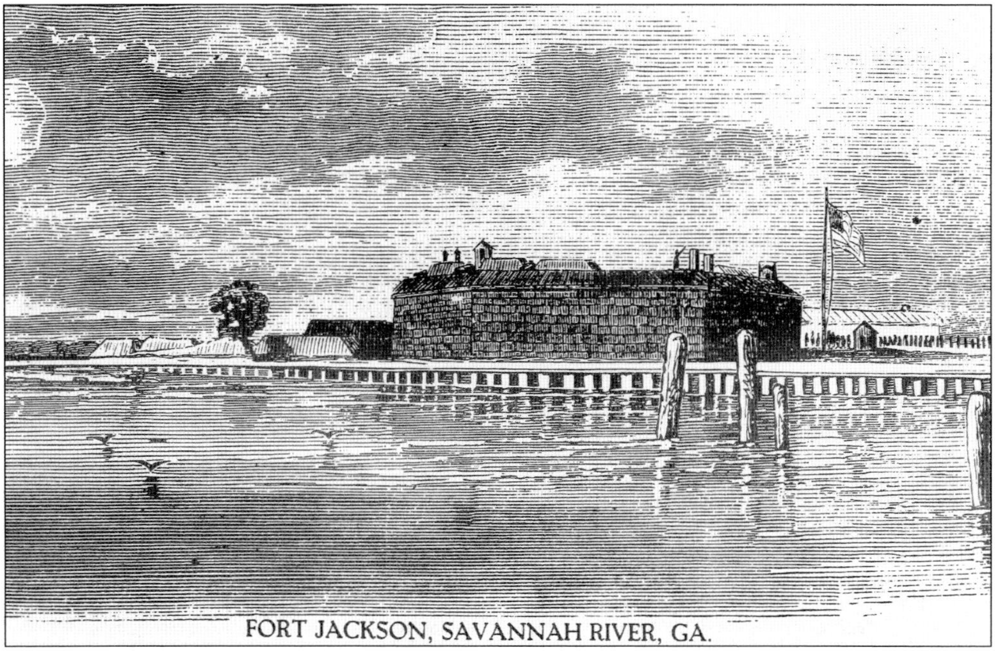

FORT JACKSON, SAVANNAH RIVER, GA.

This illustration shows Fort Jackson and Battery Lee from the Savannah River, much as they would have been seen from the CSS *Georgia*. Also evident are the wooden pilings driven into the river. These pilings, in addition to underwater torpedoes and iron-tipped obstructions, made navigation up the river extremely difficult. (Courtesy of the City of Savannah Municipal Archives.)

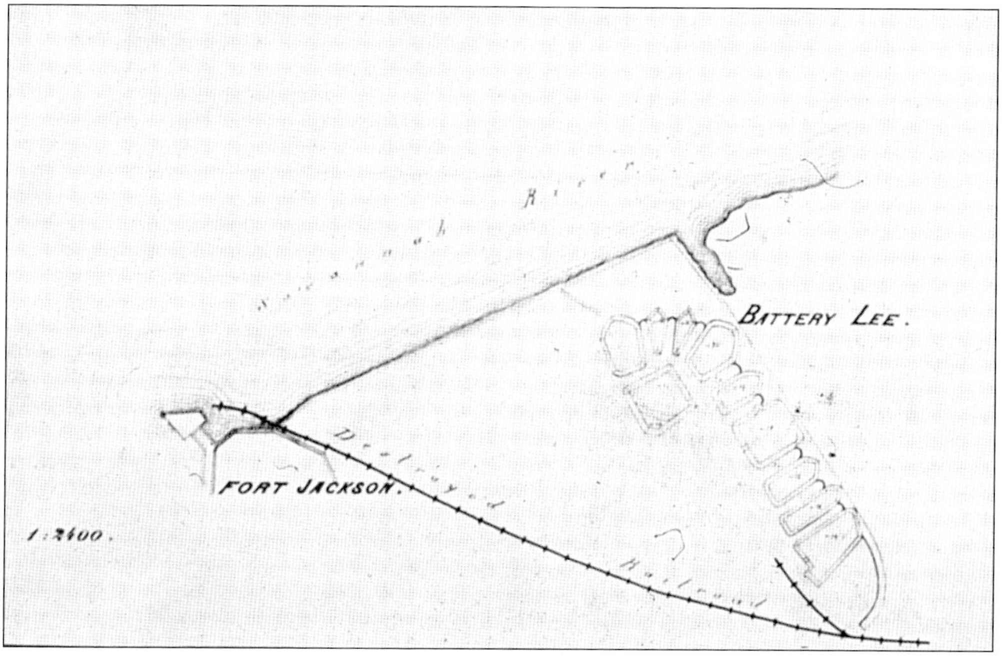

This map of Battery Lee is an inset from a large-scaled drawing, which included a plan view and sections of Fort Jackson. The map was drawn in December 1865 to go with Captain Suter's report. In the winter of 1862–1863, a spur railroad was built to Battery Lee and Fort Jackson to bring ammunition and other supplies. The train was nicknamed the "sand train" because it also hauled sand from the nearby Deptford Mounds, a Native American archaeology site. The sand was used to maintain the constantly eroding earthen embankments. The photograph below shows Battery Lee as it looked in the mid-1930s.

REBEL BATTERIES NEAR

HE DEFENCES OF SAVANNAH—THE REBEL RAM GEORGIA, AND OBSTRUCTIONS PLACED IN THE SAVANNAH RIVER, AT ELBA IS

This image from *Frank Leslie's Illustrated Newspaper* is dated February 21, 1866. The above image is an unnamed battery, but it could be Battery Lee or also one of the smaller batteries that were on both sides of the Savannah River. The image below depicts some of the river obstructions, including wooden pilings that were used to block the river and prevent the Union navy from advancing and seizing Savannah. Underwater obstructions such as mines and torpedoes were used as well. These would have been invisible and deadly in the dark water. The CSS *Georgia* is also pictured on the left side.

A piece of a cannon rises from the Wilmington River in January 2000. This area of Causton's Bluff was the location of Fort Bartow and sets the scene for a local legend. There are two sources for this story: William Mackall's 1930 memoir of his father and William Basinger's unpublished manuscript on the Savannah Volunteer Guards's history from 1858 to 1882. According to both, an experimental, very large cannon was first fired here in March 1862; however, the sources also differ from each other significantly. In Mackall's version, the cannon exploded, and the top half was thrown overhead and into the swamp behind the observers, nearly killing Gen. Robert E. Lee, who was inspecting the coastal forts. The implied question being, how would the war have been different without General Lee? Basinger does not mention General Lee but writes that several soldiers were killed and others wounded.

Archaeologist Larry Babits believes that while both writers are describing the same incident, ironically, they are not writing about the gun that was recovered and conserved. The piece recovered is about one-quarter of a cannon, not half as in Mackall's version. Babits's measurements indicate the gun recovered is a 10-inch Columbiad smooth bore, which does not match the historical records' description of a huge gun that could fire a cannonball five miles, as both authors describe. Fort Bartow did not have a 10-inch Columbiad until nearly the end of the war, if at all. The recovered cannon piece was taken to Fort Jackson for conservation. Here, staff lower the cannon into a tub for electrolysis, a conservation process that removes encrusted materials and salts from the metal by passing an electric current through the object. This cleans the object and restores it, halting further damage and oxidation.

On October 31, 1863, Pres. Jefferson Davis visited Savannah, touring the Savannah River defenses on the steamer *Beauregard* and receiving a 21-gun salute from Fort Jackson's soldiers. Some of those soldiers included the 22nd Battalion Georgia Heavy Artillery, formed November 26, 1862. The 22nd Battalion served at many of the Savannah River batteries, and Company A was among the fort's last Confederate garrisons who evacuated on December 20, 1864. The 22nd Battalion Company A was revived as a reenactors group. Dressed in period clothing, men and women volunteered their time to reenact military drills and everyday life at the fort. These volunteers often helped in other ways as well such as building structures and raising money.

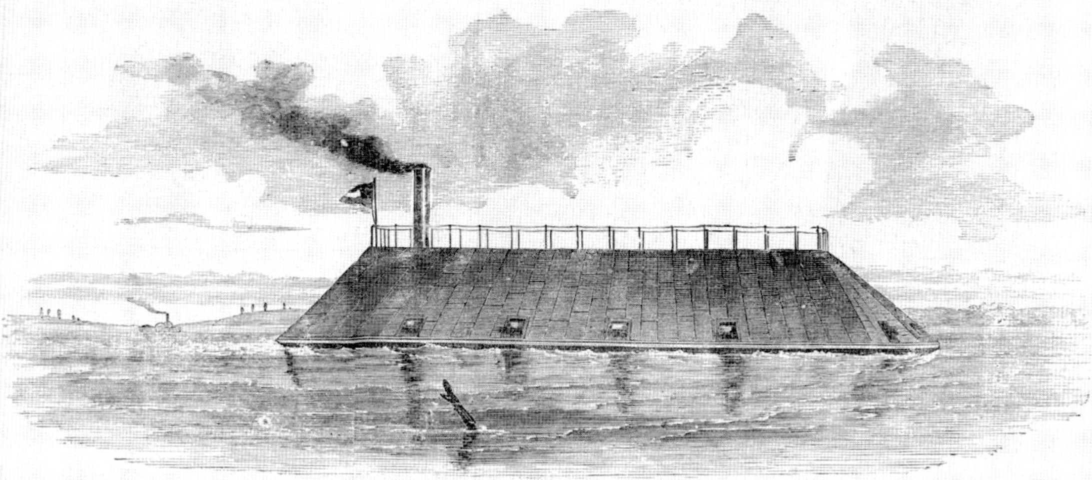

THE CONFEDERATE IRONCLAD RAM "GEORGIA."

This December 1862 *Frank Leslie's Illustrated Almanac* illustration depicts the CSS *Georgia,* which was built at Harding's Shipyard on Savannah's eastern edge. The Ladies Gunboat Association quickly raised the money, and the CSS *Georgia* was launched on May 19, 1862. The vessel was one of the new ironclads, ships with a low profile, shallow draught, and protective iron plating over every inch that rose above the water. While plate iron was the preferred material for ironcladding, none was available for the *Georgia,* so local railroad tracks were interlocked over the surface of the vessel. There is very little historical information about the design and construction of the CSS *Georgia,* which makes the archaeological evidence invaluable. It is known that the *Georgia* was seriously underpowered and had a top speed of two knots under full steam. This was inadequate to even fight the Savannah River tides. So the ship was anchored off Fort Jackson as a floating battery with guns aimed downstream. The engine ran continuously to bail water because the *Georgia* leaked terribly.

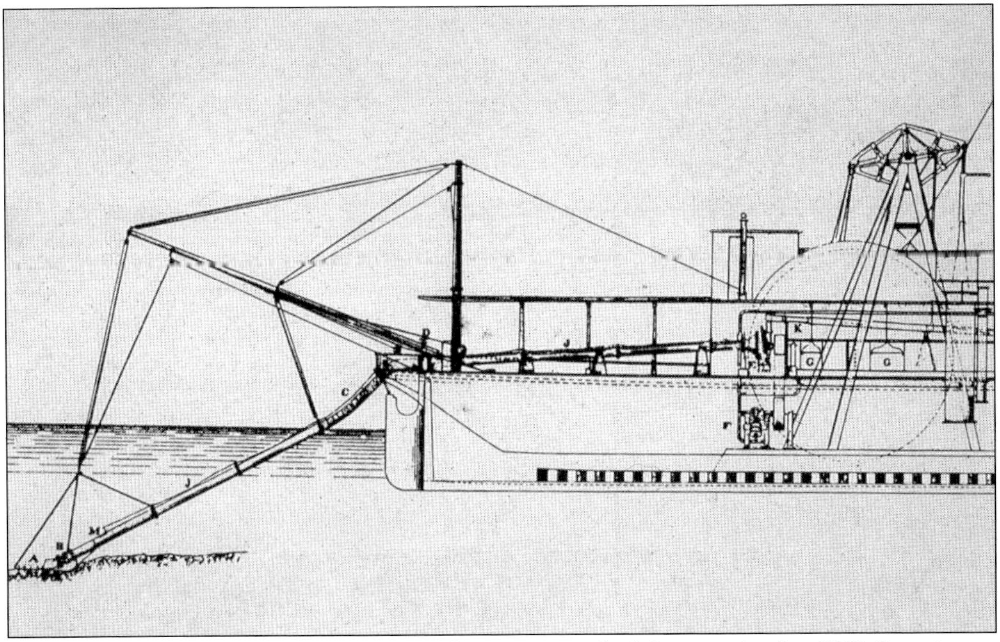

As Union general William T. Sherman's forces approached Savannah, the CSS *Georgia* was scuttled and sunk the night of December 20, 1864. Her sailors evacuated to South Carolina via steamship, along with Fort Jackson's crew. In 1868, Henry Welles dynamited the ship, and 80 tons of iron was recovered and sold through a contract with the US Treasury Department. Pictured above is a dredge ship, similar to what would have been used to retrieve materials from the *Georgia*. The *Georgia* was forgotten again until 1968 when dredge operations clearing the shipping channel "rediscovered" the vessel. Within the next decade, it was acknowledged that dredging operations were negatively affecting the wreck, and archaeological studies commenced with archaeologists working from barges (below).

Texas A&M University archaeologists conducted several archaeological and engineering assessments starting in 1979, after multiple dredging operations had impacted the *Georgia*. Working from this barge, they found an archaeology site 300 by 150 feet that was elevated seven to nine feet above the river bottom. Sections of armor plate, hull, and deck areas appeared intact, and the site had good artifact preservation. Two cannons were removed: a 32-pounder reworked as a rifled gun and a 24-pounder howitzer. Brooke rifle projectiles (pictured at right), percussion fuses, and spherical shot were also recovered and preserved. Some of these objects are now on display at the Savannah History Museum.

Coastal Heritage Society (CHS), the nonprofit that manages Old Fort Jackson, has long taken an advocacy role in protecting the CSS *Georgia* and supporting the archaeological investigations. CHS took the lead in rallying letter writing campaigns and interfacing with the Army Corps of Engineers, who are responsible for the ironclad. Each dive has used Fort Jackson as a staging ground, and the fort docks were used to load and unload materials. Above, CHS staffer John Roberson assists in safely getting the 24-pound howitzer to dry land. Roberson also conserved many of the cannons and ordnance recovered from the CSS *Georgia* over the years using specially built big tanks (below). Other materials were conserved at Fort Pulaski.

John Roberson tests the water surrounding the CSS *Georgia* cannons undergoing conservation. During electrolysis, the cannons soak in water that is a very mild solution of sodium carbonate or sodium bicarbonate (baking soda). A stronger solution means more electricity can flow through the system, so maintaining a stable balance is critical. While there are many ways to conserve iron, electrolysis remains the cheapest and easiest.

Divers prepare to enter the water. The Savannah River has extreme tides, with the water rising and falling up to 10 feet with each change from low to high tide or vice versa. Consequently, currents in the river are very swift, so archaeologists can usually only work at high or low tide but not in between.

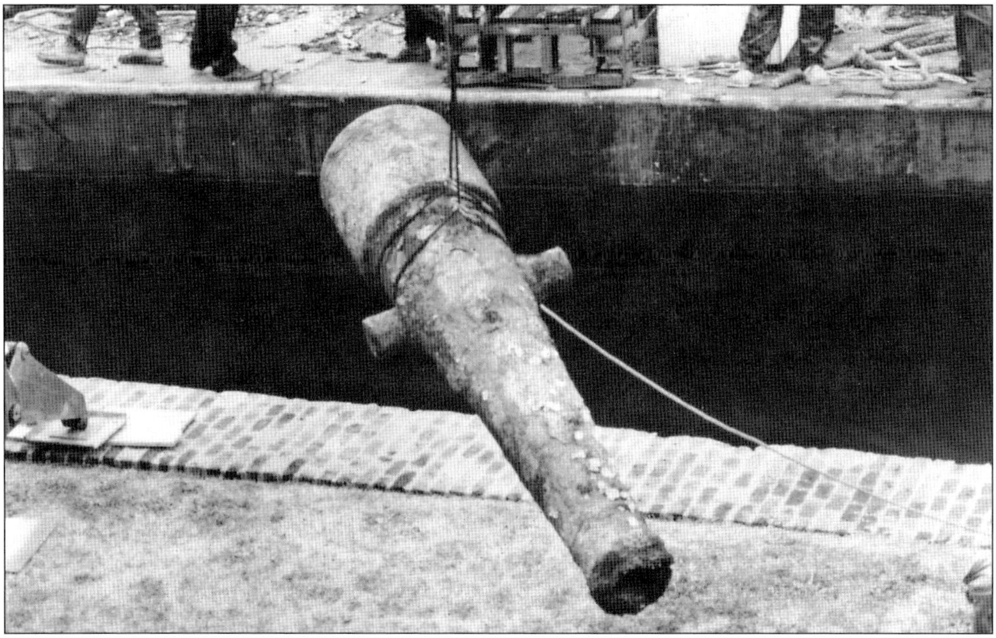

The other cannon that was removed early from the wreck was a 32-pounder modified into a 6.4-inch rifled cannon that would have fired Brooke projectiles. Modifications include a spiral groove on the inside to "rifle" it and a band around the widest end, which reinforced and strengthened the cannon so it could handle larger ordnance. Here, the cannon is transferred via crane from the barge to Fort Jackson to undergo cleaning and conservation. This cannon is marked with a "32" over "1852" on the right trunnion, or pivot point for aiming the cannon, indicating this cannon was made in 1852. The left trunnion reads "P" over "CWS."

Every artifact recovered from an underwater site must undergo conservation after being submerged. Conservation can take years for iron cannons that were submerged in saltwater or a few days for glass or ceramic artifacts. Pictured here clockwise from top left are a carpenter's adze, probably the ship's carpenter's tool; a wine bottle base; an ironstone serving dish; leg shackles for punishing misbehaving sailors; and a large nut and bolt.

The Savannah River's brackish, silty water has nearly zero visibility. Archaeologists working on the wreck often wore helmets with air supplied from the surface and were able to talk to workers on the surface. Here, Dr. J. Alan May operates the communications for the air hat dives. He is likely speaking to Rik Anuskiewicz, who is underwater using a Superlite 17 light air helmet.

After the war, the smaller batteries were dismantled and the difficult task of removing river obstructions began. In addition to the CSS *Georgia* salvage, which helped to clear the shipping channel, mines, wooden pilings, and other obstructions had to be removed so shipping and commerce could restart. From the city's founding to this day, Savannah's port has always been a

THE SAVANNAH RIVER, GA., BELOW FORT JACKSON.

critical component of the economy. This restoration process would take several years. The Army Corps' chief of engineers reported in 1873 that the project was nearly complete except for removing two wooden shipwrecks near Fort Pulaski and some dredging in that area.

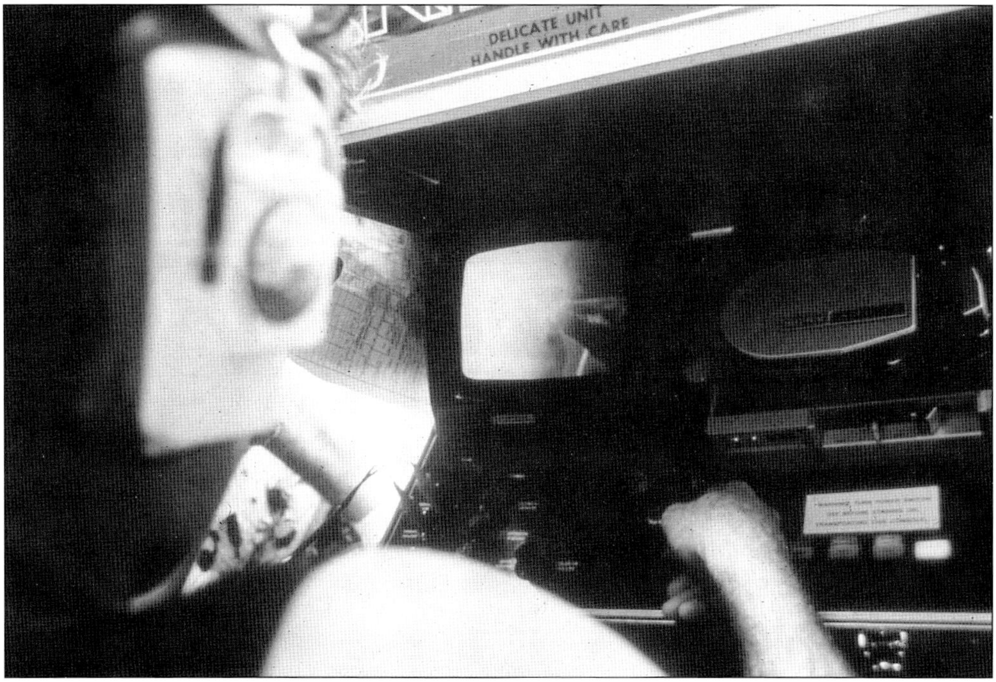

Above is likely Tom York, a marine biologist and diver for the Army Corps of Engineers, Savannah District. He is operating an underwater video camera via remote control to get close-up footage of the wreck. Technology has improved greatly since these grainy pictures were taken. In 2013, archaeologists mapped the site with high-resolution multibeam and side-scan sonar surveys. These precise maps allowed researchers floating on a barge above the wreck to direct archaeologists underwater working by feel in the dark. Below, divers prepare to enter the water. This diver wears SCUBA gear and lacks a dive helmet that allows underwater contact with the surface.

Four

Outdated then Abandoned

The 100-Year Wait (1865–1965)

After the Civil War, the US military faced a conundrum: rifled technology had made all forts obsolete and therefore inconsequential. Shortly thereafter, Fort Jackson was only receiving periodic maintenance. Except for use as a port quarantine station in 1867, then a brief attempt at modernization in the 1870s, Fort Jackson was attended by a keeper until 1905 when it was officially abandoned. Then it would sit vacant.

In 1884, Fort Jackson's name was changed to Fort Oglethorpe to avoid confusion with Fort Jackson in South Carolina. That year, Congress only appropriated $480 for very basic maintenance and the keeper. During the Spanish-American War in April 1898, the fort's guns were removed, but in the process, two fell into the moat and had to be salvaged with barges.

Fort Jackson regained its historic name in 1905 to avoid confusion with another Fort Oglethorpe, an active military base in northern Georgia founded in 1902. In 1923, Congress declared Fort Jackson surplus property and put it up for sale. The City of Savannah purchased the property with the intent to create a park. However, the Great Depression and World War II delayed those plans. In the early 1940s, Southeastern Shipyards bought the property and made Liberty ships and mine sweepers for the war effort. This area east of Savannah has continued to be industrial. In 1955, American Cyanamid Company bought Fort Jackson and the surrounding area. The company tried to get interest in Fort Jackson as a historic site, offering to sell it for $1, but could not get any takers after several years. So the company threatened to dismantle the fort for scrap. This tactic worked, and Judge Alexander Lawrence and other Savannah citizens lobbied the state to buy it. In 1965, the Georgia Historical Commission (predecessor of today's Historic Preservation Division) bought the property and began planning for a maritime heritage museum.

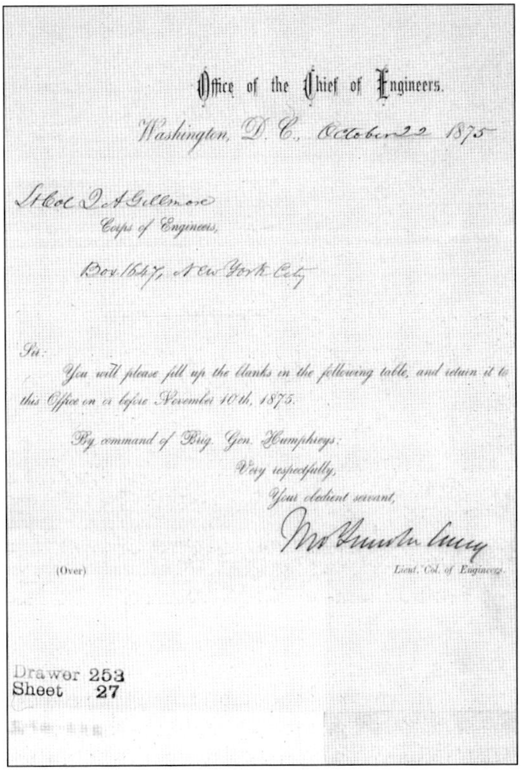

Office of the Chief of Engineers.

Washington, D. C., October 22 1875

Lt Col Q A Gillmore
Corps of Engineers,

Box 1647, New York City

Sir:

You will please fill up the blanks in the following table, and return it to this Office on or before November 10th, 1875.

By command of Brig. Gen. Humphreys:

Very respectfully,

Your obedient servant,

[illegible signature]

Lieut. Col. of Engineers.

(Over)

Drawer 253
Sheet 27

The early 1870s brought new plans to ready and rehabilitate Fort Jackson. Proposals included increasing the wall's thickness, adding guns to the east wall, strengthening the powder magazine, and mounting 15-inch caliber guns, which weighed 25 tons each. These October 1875 documents show Fort Jackson had three 10-inch Rodman guns and two 100-pounder Parrot rifles already mounted with five 15-inch guns in progress. The work was slow and piecemeal. Eventually, work stopped on all forts in 1877. At this point, a caretaker was appointed. His job was to guard the structure and the government property stored inside while he lived in the casemates and dealt with the mosquitoes and drunk fishermen.

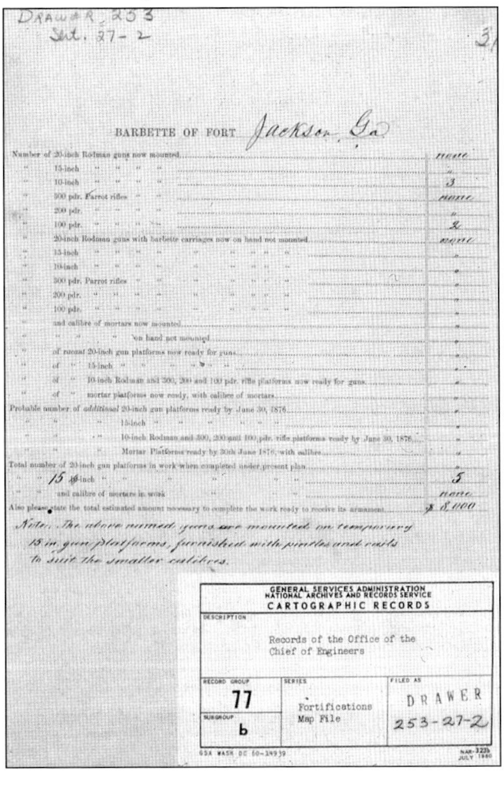

DRAWER 253
Sht. 27-2

3

BARBETTE OF FORT Jackson, Ga

Number of 20-inch Rodman guns now mounted	none
" 15-inch " " " "	"
" 10-inch " " " "	3
" 300 pdr. Parrot rifles " "	none
" 200 pdr. " " " "	"
" 100 pdr. " " " "	2
" 20-inch Rodman guns with barbette carriages now on hand not mounted	none
" 15-inch " " " " " " " " "	"
" 10-inch " " " " " " " " "	"
" 300 pdr. Parrot rifles " " " " " " "	"
" 200 pdr. " " " " " " " " "	"
" 100 pdr. " " " " " " " " "	"
" and calibre of mortars now mounted	"
" " " " on hand not mounted	"
" of vacant 20-inch gun platforms now ready for guns	"
" of " 15-inch " " " " "	"
" of " 10-inch Rodman and 300, 200 and 100 pdr. rifle platforms now ready for guns	"
" of " mortar platforms now ready, with calibre of mortars	"
Probable number of *additional* 20-inch gun platforms ready by June 30, 1876	"
" " " 15-inch " " " " " "	"
" " " 10-inch Rodman and 300, 200 and 100 pdr. rifle platforms ready by June 30, 1876	"
" " " Mortar Platforms ready by 30th June 1876, with calibre	"
Total number of 20-inch gun platforms in work when completed under present plan	"
" " 15 inch " " " " " "	5
" " and calibre of mortars in work " " "	none
Also please state the total estimated amount necessary to complete the work ready to receive its armament	$ 8,000

Note. The above named guns are mounted on temporary 15 in. gun platforms, furnished with pintles and rails to suit the smaller calibres.

GENERAL SERVICES ADMINISTRATION
NATIONAL ARCHIVES AND RECORDS SERVICE
CARTOGRAPHIC RECORDS

DESCRIPTION: Records of the Office of the Chief of Engineers

RECORD GROUP: 77
SUBGROUP: b
SERIES: Fortifications Map File
FILED AS: DRAWER 253-27-2

Documentary photographer William Ernest Wilson took these pictures sometime between 1883 and 1893 while a resident of Savannah. Above, both magazines and two cannons are visible above the parapet. Also note that the sally port and entry doors are painted white. In the foreground, the field is torn up and a low berm runs east–west. Below is the fort as it meets the Savannah River. The different layers of brick are visible in the front wall: lower courses of small Savannah grey bricks, then long thin Savannah greys in English bond, and the uppermost section of jumbo greys in common bond dating to the 1840s renovations. At least two rows of wooden pilings that supported the wooden deck are still present (Courtesy of Hargrett Rare Book and Manuscript Library/University of Georgia Libraries.)

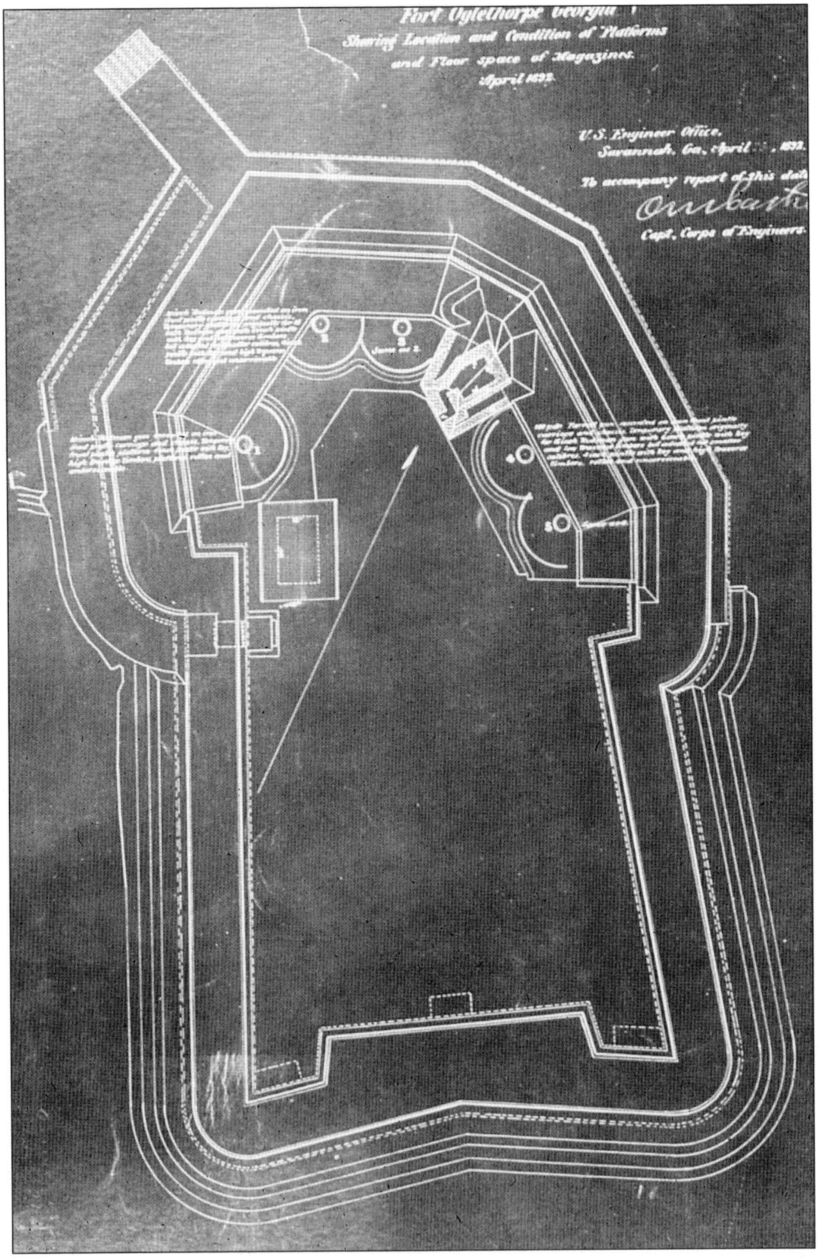

This map is labeled "Fort Oglethorpe Georgia, Showing Location and Condition of Platforms and Floor Space of Magazines, April 1892." The new shell magazine is outlined in very thick white lines at the gun platform's northeastern corner. This magazine was built around 1873 and differs from the powder magazine because it held prepared shells preloaded with gunpowder. For obvious reasons, military regulations stipulated that black powder and prepared shells be housed separately. The 1870s attempts to recondition Fort Jackson also included a new wharf, temporary buildings for housing, and five platforms for the new heavy guns, marked by white semicircles and numbered. By 1892, all work on Fort Jackson had ceased. This map was part of the yearly inspections and reports as the government's focus shifted to the river channel, and the fort was used to store materials for harbor projects.

The first half of the 20th century was a very quiet time for Fort Jackson. Around 1935, Savannah's mayor requested the National Park Service study Fort Jackson and consider making it an "outlying unit" of Fort Pulaski National Monument. Fort Pulaski staff, including Supt. Ralston Lattimore, visited Fort Jackson, taking pictures, studying the site's history, and judging the site's significance. The following five pages feature pictures taken during this visit. The above picture shows the sally port, overgrown moat, and general state of the jungle that engulfed Fort Jackson at the time. Below is the sally port and powder magazine, looking out from the parade ground.

The photograph at left shows the details of the sally port; the Savannah grey brickwork, red sandstone lintels above the loopholes, and gray-white granite are in excellent condition. The stone cross beams for the wooden drawbridge are present, but the drawbridge itself has rotted away. The sally port is in the Gothic Revival architectural style. William Mitchell Jr. wrote on the fort's National Register of Historic Places nomination that the sally port's crenellated decoration is an exception to the "otherwise severely unadorned structure whose brutal beauty derives from handsome Savannah Grey brickwork." Below, getting to the fort was difficult, and the only access was by boat. Fort Pulaski staff appear to have used a rickety ladder leaned against the tide tunnel to access the structure for evaluation.

These two photographs were likely taken from the same location along the northeast corner of the outer moat wall. The first view is looking west toward Savannah with two men standing on the tide tunnel. The moat intake tunnel is just barely visible above the vegetation. The second picture was taken facing south along the outer eastern wall. The moat was originally just a ditch surrounding the fort. When the fort was upgraded in the 1850s, the moat was formalized into a 20-foot-wide, seven-foot-deep moat with a brick counterscarp wall forming the outer moat and a drawbridge to cross the moat at the sally port.

National Park Service historian Rogers W. Young wrote a short report in October 1936 evaluating Fort Jackson's potential as a park. Young noted the fort's beauty and excellent physical condition, describing it as "practically undamaged" and writing that there was no need for historic preservation. However, even while acknowledging its early construction date, Young dismissed Fort Jackson's historic importance, writing that a "museum is not thought necessary." This determination was primarily because Fort Jackson was not involved in any battles, while he ignored the contributions made as Savannah's sentry. Despite this initial dismissal, Fort Jackson was listed in the National Register of Historic Places in 1970 and became a National Historic Landmark in 2000. Below, the overgrown fort blends into the landscape as seen from Battery Lee.

The moat is seen at low tide around 1935. While the great majority of the fort was in excellent condition, some damage can be seen. For instance, in the lower left of this photograph, bricks have been dislodged at the corner. The foliage growing into the brick is also doing damage as the roots invade the soft mortar, breaking it up.

This nearly unrecognizable part of the fort is the interior eastern wall of the battery. The c. 1873 shell magazine is barely visible at top left. The striking shadows indicate that this photograph was taken on a sunny day; however, the darkness resulting from overgrowth contrasts sharply with today's open parade ground.

Battery Lee was in surprisingly good repair around 1935. The picture below gives perspective on the height of the battery when compared to the man standing at the base. Earthen embankments are very prone to erosion, hence the need for the Civil War "sand train" to continually maintain the battery. Unlike the fort's masonry, however, the vegetation and trees are helpful in maintaining an earthen embankment. The roots help anchor the soil in place while the ground cover prevents the top layers from washing away. Today, Battery Lee is on private property and is not open to the public or available for visitation.

While the fort sat unoccupied, intrepid individuals would occasionally explore the fort for shelter or for fun. Pictured at right is Dr. Martha Fay, a highly respected Savannah educator who taught biology and chemistry at Armstrong College in the 1940s. She was also an activist serving on the Savannah Chatham Board of Education, Chatham Board of Health, and League of Women Voters' Savannah Branch. Dr. Fay explored the fort in 1947 with her husband, Dr. Richard Fay (below), who was a research entomologist at Oatland Island's US Public Health Service laboratory. Their daughter Libby Fay recalled her parents telling stories of their explorations, noting that they found lots of poison ivy at the fort.

The Fays loved to explore the area in their mahogany canoe and likely took the above picture from their canoe in 1947. Below, this 1963 aerial picture shows the fort at the center with Battery Lee beyond and the American Cyanamid Company in the background. Two years before the State of Georgia purchased Fort Jackson, the fort had a forest within its walls, but directly to the west, the adjacent field is eroding due to the deepening of the Savannah River channel. On the fort's eastern side, a double line of pilings is visible sticking up above the river. These are the remaining supports for the railroad and the wood decking.

Five

Historic Preservation and Archaeology

Retrieving the Past

The State of Georgia bought Fort Jackson in 1965, and the now-defunct Georgia Historical Commission (GHC) immediately began to restore the fort. However, the intent was not to interpret Fort Jackson itself. Instead, the fort housed a maritime history museum, unimaginatively named the Fort Jackson Maritime Museum. GHC staff began by clearing the overgrowth from the fort, and Gunn Meyerhoff, a local architectural firm, built several modern support buildings and an extension from the casemates into the parade ground to house the new museum. This addition, the subsequent utilities installation, and the support work prompted one Fort Jackson staff member to later write, albeit from the advantage of hindsight, "The most destructive force ever to besiege Fort Jackson was not the British or Union military forces, but rather the Georgia Historical Commission. The construction of a maritime museum in the casemates of the fort has done even more damage than the attack of the CSS *Savannah*." The new construction caused the fort's structure to be gutted, altering and damaging the archaeological record when additional footing and utilities were laid. Of course, the state's goal was not preserving the fort, it was building a new museum. The barracks' foundations fared better. They were capped with Savannah grey bricks in the 1960s, and then in 1973, the parade ground was backfilled to match the foundation level, creating a flat surface and eliminating the trip hazard of raised foundations.

The maritime museum was closed due to budget cuts in the fall of 1975 after less than 10 years of operation. The next year, the nonprofit Coastal Heritage Society (CHS) was formed, and it entered into a long-term lease to manage, interpret, and preserve Old Fort Jackson. CHS reopened the fort on Labor Day in 1976 and has been managing it ever since.

The fort is seen from the Savannah River in August 1965. Note the wood pilings running the length of the fort. Original construction drawings show a wood deck spanning the counterscarp, or outer moat walls, to the pilings, allowing for more walkable surface in front of the fort. Evidence suggests these pilings were added in 1857, when the counterscarp was built. The pilings' purpose was to form a retaining wall protecting the fort. More pilings extend to the east (left side), which supported the Confederate rail line. The State of Georgia removed the old pilings and the Confederate railroad between 1965 and 1970, primarily for aesthetic reasons. Once removed, workers saw the original carpentry marks and could determine the cypress pilings were hand hewn to a pointed tip and had vertical sash sawn markings. The preservation was excellent because the pilings were driven into the mud, an anaerobic (oxygen-free) environment. Without oxygen, tiny marine organisms that eat wood and other organic material could not survive.

The fort's interior as viewed from the gun platform's eastern side shows the casemates below the gun platform and the Savannah River in the distance. The 1870s shell magazine is on the right side. This picture dates to August 1965, when the staff had begun clearing vegetation. While large trees are still present, the fort's features can now be discerned.

By December 1965, the work on Fort Jackson was rapidly progressing. A temporary dirt road took the place of a drawbridge, and work commenced on the brickwork. A pile of recovered bricks is stacked at the interior of the sally port. Note the damage and missing brick along the corners of the sally port.

Above is the interior of the parade ground with much of the larger plants and trees removed; however, there is still much work to be done to make the parade ground "tourist friendly" and accessible to visitors. The southeast corner is pictured, and on either side of the right tree, the ghost outline of walls can be seen extending one-half to two-thirds up the outer wall. These smaller walls are from one of three privies along the fort's rear. While the vegetation cleared from the fort's interior makes a dramatic difference, the moat (below) would remain full for another five years until being cleared.

The *Cruz Del Sur* sails on her first voyage up the Savannah River, passing Fort Jackson in 1965. Some of the vegetation has been removed from the fort's interior, and some barracks' foundations are visible. Built in 1947 at Valencia, Spain, the *Cruz del Sur* is a 158-foot, three masted barkentine with a 150-ton burden and an auxiliary diesel engine. After briefly operating as a Spanish training ship, the boat was purchased by Twentieth Century Fox and was used in the filming of the 1965 movie *High Wind in Jamaica*, starring Anthony Quinn and James Coburn. Mills B. Lane Jr. purchased the vessel in 1965 and docked it outside of the Ships of the Sea Museum, located at the time along Savannah's River Street. For the next several years, the ship only made small trips along the Savannah River while it underwent extensive repairs and refitting, including work on the hull and interior, new masts, and a new engine.

Unlike removing vegetation from the parade ground, which is relatively simple, removing vegetation with roots that have invaded the masonry is much more difficult. The damage from the vegetation is obvious along this wall (above), and unless caution is used, preservationists removing plants can cause even more damage, such as pulling out mortar and even whole bricks along with the invasive roots. Below, this photograph shows the western scarp and dates to 1966 when more progress has been made unveiling the fort. A modern dock has been installed next to the tide tunnel, which is hidden behind the palm tree.

Above is an undated photograph found in a Savannah-area antique store around 2001. The substantial tree growth and men's suits suggest the first half of the 20th century, but it is difficult to be more specific. The original is a three-by-four-inch snapshot. At right is a similar perspective, taken in December 1965. The large tree has been removed, the ground at the base shows evidence of disturbance, and planks have been placed to mitigate the mud. The top three to four rows of bricks have been damaged, probably cut back to accommodate the new addition. (Above, courtesy of Jefferson Reed.)

These two views of the fort's landward side show the moat clogged with vegetation and rice fields continuing to surround the fort. These rice plants are descendants from the rice plantations, which were critical to Savannah's early wealth. Enslaved people worked the rice plantations, engineering and constructing elaborate irrigation ditches, levees, and gates to flood the fields at specific times. Farming rice fields required extensive specialized knowledge as well as immensely difficult physical labor. Historically, the river was freshwater here and could be used to flood the fields; however, today, the Savannah River flowing past Fort Jackson is brackish. This changed with the deepening of the harbor.

This is a close-up view of the interior sally port. Here, a mechanism of winding, ratcheted chains and counterweights opened and closed the drawbridge. Typically, the counterweights were positioned so when released, their weight lifted the drawbridge. To lower the bridge, the counterweights were ratcheted back into place with levers. The stone is Vermont white-gray granite.

The Georgia Historical Commission built this archaeology lab, which was used for basic archaeological lab work and conservation, such as washing artifacts, drying and re-bagging objects, and analysis. The building, which was constructed with prefabricated "logs" and assembled on-site, was later was used as a residence for staff but is no longer standing.

Dr. William Kelso conducted archaeology at Fort Jackson between November 20, 1967, and January 28, 1968. The project had three goals: to solve drainage problems, learn about the construction and consequent destruction periods in the 19th century, and understand 19th-century military life at the fort. Two main areas were targeted, a sunken area in the center of the parade ground and the privies along the back wall. The central area, dug first, turned out to be a 13-foot-deep well lined with wood planks and bricks near the base. The southern half of the well had collapsed and filled with modern materials. Few artifacts were found except the wooden ring and bricks stabilizing the bottom. Pictured above is the excavation in progress. Below is a close-up of the well during excavation.

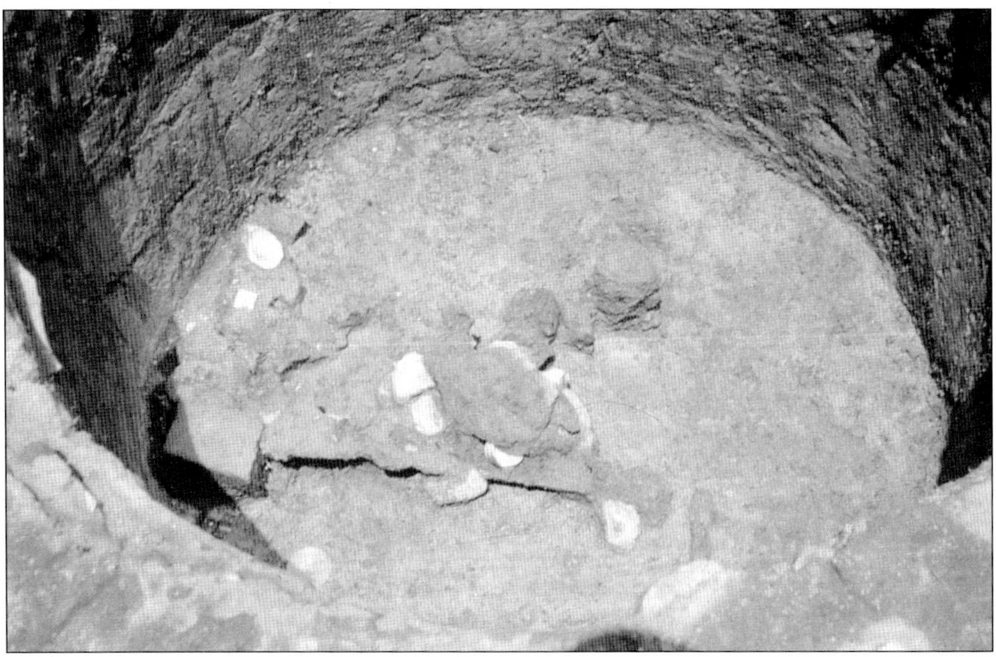

All soil removed from a dig site is typically screened or put through a wire mesh that allows the soil to fall through while catching artifacts. Sometimes, especially in wet environments or with clay, the soil will be screened using a flow of water as well. This technique is rather obviously called "wet screening" and usually is as simple as hosing down the soil in the screen, as seen here. Fancier configurations are sometimes used where a larger screen with a quarter inch mesh is stacked over top a smaller screen (like a window screen). This allows archaeologists to recover tiny, delicate items such as straight pins, fish scales, and beads.

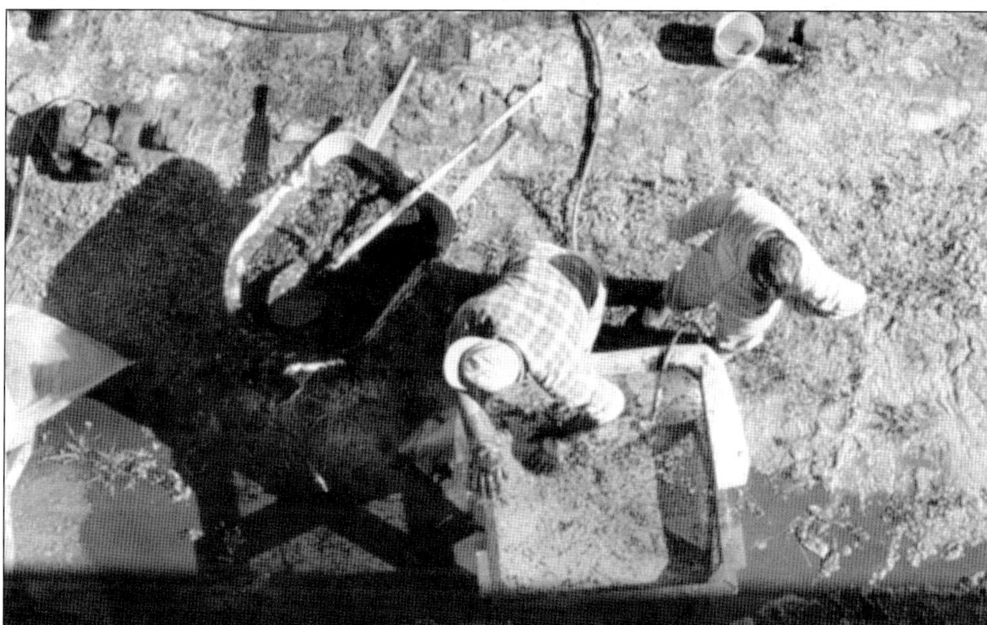

Privies, or outhouses, are often key areas where artifacts collect. This is for two reasons. One, they are often generally used for trash disposal, and, two, if something accidentally falls in, it is rarely recovered (for obvious reasons). Fort Jackson's privies, located at the two back corners and centrally along the back wall, had small drainage tunnels into the moat, so the tide carried away waste twice daily. The evidence, including contemporary maps, the artifacts recovered, and architectural details such as the ventilators built into the fort's back wall, all suggest these privies were built between 1842 and 1844 at the same time as the back wall. During the 1960s excavations, two of the central vaults and one vault in the fort's southeastern corner were excavated. Thousands of artifacts were recovered detailing the 19th-century lives of the people who lived there.

An animal bone and the top of a wine bottle lie in situ, or in place, in the excavation. Zooarchaeologists analyze animal bone to understand what people were eating (pork, chicken, fish, and venison) and what cuts of meat were used. For example, were inhabitants eating big steaks or cheaper, tough cuts of meat? By examining cut marks on bones, zooarchaeologists can determine how the animal was butchered as well.

The Fort Jackson privies held thousands of artifacts and were particularly rich in kitchen trash. The kitchen was adjacent to the central privies, providing a convenient place to dump refuse. Clockwise from top left, pictured are German Westerwald stoneware (probably a mug), an earthenware mug, a spoon, a tin-glazed earthenware plate dating to well before the fort's era, and a knife.

Some historic pottery has maker's marks, or manufacturing marks, that can tell archaeologists much about an individual piece of ceramic. Above, this maker's mark is on a stoneware jug from Trenton, South Carolina, which is near Aiken. Unfortunately, the exact manufacturer is not identifiable. The white sherd below is ironstone, a plain, white ceramic that was found in abundance at Fort Jackson. It was popular between 1840 and 1870 but was produced into the 20th century and was widely available as plates, cups, mugs, bowls, serving vessels, and pitchers. This piece has a registration mark. The coded, diamond image tells us this piece was registered on December 18, 1856, at the London patent office.

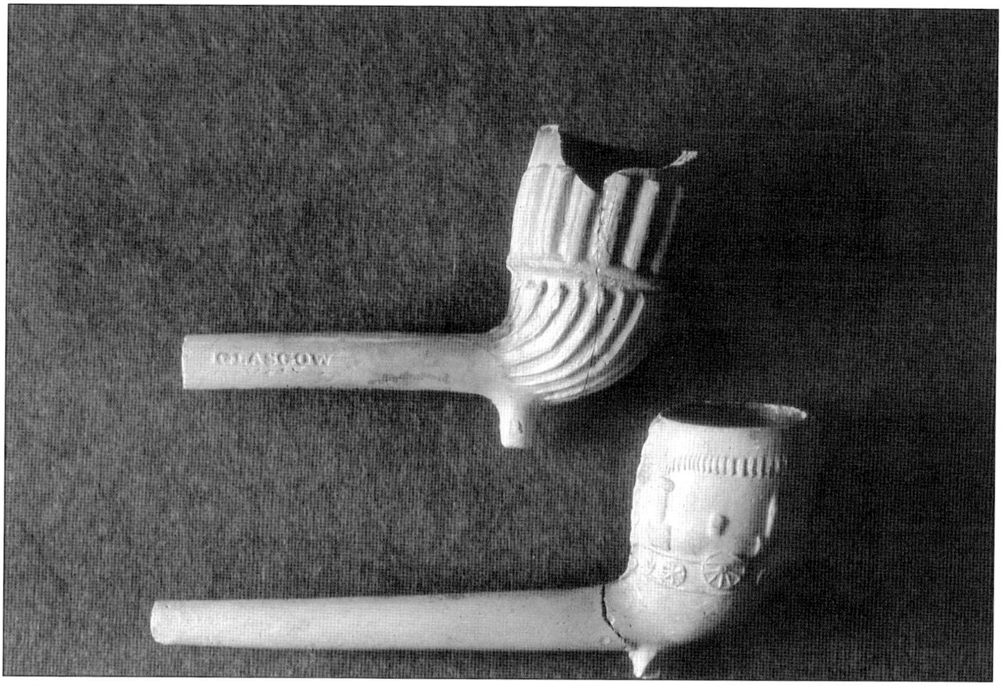

Tobacco pipes were another common find, as they broke easily and were relatively cheap entertainment. The white clay pipes (above) come in many designs and sometimes also have manufacturer's names or places. The pipe shown above was made in Glasgow, Scotland, while the pipe below has a steam engine on one side (pictured) and a side-wheeler steam boat opposite. Dr. William Kelso suggested this image commemorated the 50th anniversary of steam power. Two less common reed stem pipes were also recovered (below). These are clay pipes that would have been fitted with a replaceable "reed" stem. On the left is a simpler molded and crosshatch design. The right side has a molded human head and face but is incomplete.

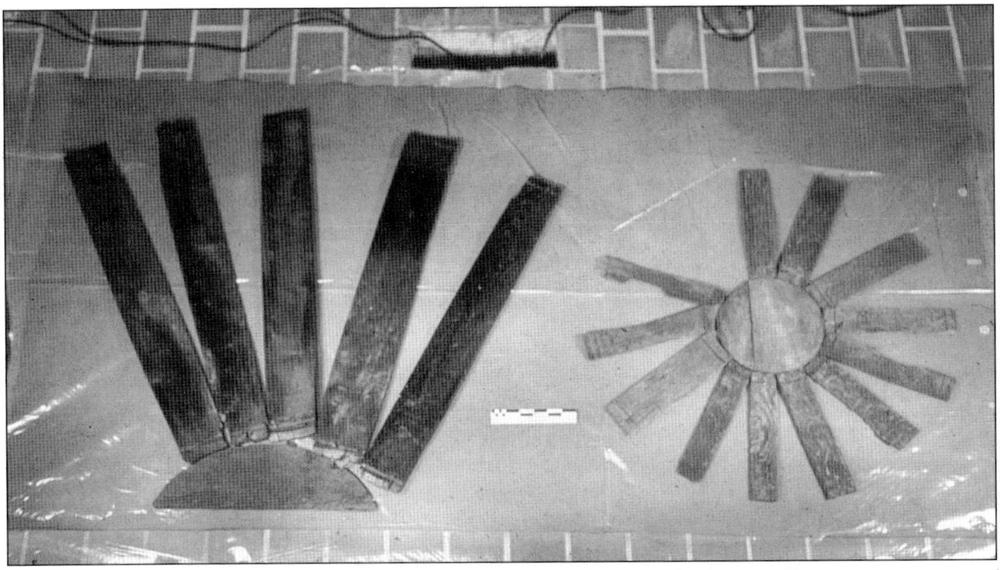

The extremely wet environment in the privies' lower layers made for excellent preservation of organic materials like plant seeds and wood, which normally decompose quickly in Georgia's hot, humid environment. These are portions of the four barrels and one small powder keg that were found in the privies. One barrel was cut in half, and Dr. Kelso suggested this was used as a makeshift chair.

The waterlogged environment also allowed for leather preservation. Thirty-five shoes were found, including one woman's shoe and two high-button children's shoes. These shoes are compelling evidence that sometimes whole families lived at the fort. Women are extremely rare in the fort's documentary evidence. Archaeology provides a critical, complementary data set to the written record.

By December 1968, most of the State of Georgia's work was complete to transform Old Fort Jackson from wilderness into a historic site. The interior parade ground was cleared and had grass growing. Original building foundations were uncovered and visible, and the archaeologists had solved the immediate flooding issues (right). The museum and brick staircase to the gun platform were complete, and a concrete floor was added to the gun platform. Careful observers will note the lack of a handrail in the picture below. Other images also show this section of the gun platform without any safety measures, although a handrail exists elsewhere along the gun platform.

Perched on the river, Fort Jackson has been subject to flooding for most of its existence. Starting in the late 1940s, dredging the river's shipping channel has greatly exacerbated the problem, resulting in more traffic and bigger ships causing massive shoreline erosion. Side effects include damage to the fort's structure and the entire fort flooding. This Georgia Historical Commission postcard dates between 1965 and 1971. The extent of the erosion problem is evident. The pile of rocks is an unsuccessful attempt to control the erosion. On the left side, wood pilings that support the fort's foundation are visible. This is a serious problem. As long as the cypress pilings are submerged in the mud, they remain in an anaerobic environment, meaning there is no oxygen and therefore no marine organisms to eat away at the wood. Once exposed to the air and water, however, the wood pilings will quickly break down under the combined pressures of wave action, organisms like marine borers, and wind and water alternately wetting and drying out the wood causing expansion and contraction.

These photographs also document how significant the erosion problem had become between 1965 and 1971. Comparing this photograph to the 1963 aerial on page 60, one can see the maritime museum improvements are completed, and the fort's structure and modern support buildings are clearly visible. Even considering that these photographs could have been taken at different tide levels, the erosion has considerably advanced in only a few years both east and west of the fort. Other important differences to note are that the wood pilings have been removed from the river, a dock was built next to the tide tunnel, and the barracks' foundations are clearly visible in the parade ground. Modern support buildings, a parking lot, and a permanent access road are visible on the right side.

The Army Corps of Engineers, the entity in charge of the Savannah Harbor, and engineer Buddy De Young in particular, arranged for the corps to be responsible for controlling erosion around Fort Jackson. This was appropriate considering that Fort Jackson was the Army Corps' first project in the Savannah area. The first bank stabilization project was in 1971. From a floating barge, workers laid a line of "wooden mattresses," similar to large pallets, onto the riverbank and piled large stone riprap on top to a depth of two feet. Soil fill was brought in to replenish the field behind the riprap. The first stabilization project began to fail after one year as the rock slipped and water flowed behind the barrier, undermining the moat. The project was redone in 1973 and 1974 for a total cost of about $750,000.

This aerial photograph shows the riprap work in progress; the western shoreline (right side) is covered in riprap, but the eastern side is not. The brick outlines of the barracks and other interior buildings are clearly visible, as is the new museum extension and dock directly off the front of the fort.

Concurrent with the riprap placement, workers also dug out years of accumulated mud and vegetation from the moat. This was done as time allowed and equipment was available. Most of the muck was removed with a clamshell bucket on a crane. Here, the bucket goes underwater for another scoop. In the foreground are pillars for the wood drawbridge.

Once all of the mud was removed, the well-preserved wood floor at the moat's base became visible (above). Then artifacts were discovered. Frances Wilson Smith stopped the mass excavation and instructed workers to begin shoveling and hand excavating the cache of artifacts. Below, a state employee shovels the mud to uncover artifacts. Thirty projectiles (cannonballs and other ordnance), whole bottles and bottle fragments, and an entire cannon carriage wheel were found. These artifacts were attributed to Confederates fleeing Sherman's advance on December 20, 1864. It is hypothesized the soldiers pushed the materials into the moat to prevent the Union army from using them.

Fort Jackson has undergone several large projects to fix and maintain the masonry since 1965. Pictured is master mason Eluigi Perkins, who did the first repairs when the state purchased Fort Jackson. Perkins worked at the fort daily for 10 years, doing repairs and maintenance. Here, he works on a scaffolding that can be adjusted to any height by pulleys. He was later given a lifetime membership to the Coastal Heritage Society. While Perkins's work was excellent and state of the art at the time, historic preservationists have learned an enormous amount since 1965, especially about how old structures weather and "breathe" with the changes in environment.

A common early "fix" was adding iron bars to secure masonry cracks, pictured here during installation (left). However, over several decades, the iron rusts and expands, forcing the masonry to further crack apart. Later, preservationists had to remove the iron and repair the cracks again. Below, often simply called a "crack monitor," this little device does exactly that. If the masonry shifts, then the difference can be read on the graph. This older version is simple. Today's versions will record changes like a slow seismograph as well as do a better job of monitoring vertical and horizontal movement in the structure.

Both images show Fort Jackson around 1974 or 1975. By this point, the sally port had a proper bridge, even if it was not a drawbridge. The electrical pole (below) was removed in 1979 with grant money to better maintain the historic appearance. These two pictures were taken at the same time as the top picture on the next page. Someone later wrote on the back of that one, "The anchor is gone now, but this is the main entrance to the fort. The wall & windows are a 'bastardization' committed by the state in 1965. Scott's main goal is to rip out that wall & move the exhibits to a new building away from the fort proper."

The maritime museum is an example of how history and interpretations change over time. These views of the museum show how the museum's architects did their best to blend the new building with the old to create new, usable space for exhibits. Above is the museum at ground level looking north toward the river, and below is the museum from the gun platform looking away from the river. However, later interpretations focused on the fort itself, and the Coastal Heritage Society finally got its wish to remove all modern additions in the 1990s. Generally, today's historians prefer stripping away modern additions to reveal the original. This theory, of course, begs the question, what is original? Is it the War of 1812 fort? The pre–Civil War version? What about the 1873 shell magazine? Will future preservationists curse the removal of the 1960s changes?

In 1996, the Fort Jackson Maritime Museum addition was removed. Then masons had to repair where the buildings had connected (above). Today, people know it is critical to use historically appropriate materials that are as close to the original as possible. This not only returns the structure to its original appearance, but also helps the long-term structural stability. Two years after the addition's removal, the accompanying brick staircase was demolished with volunteer help, finally returning the fort largely to its later 19th-century appearance (below). The brick staircase, which protruded into the parade ground, was replaced with a metal staircase that is more unobtrusive.

Above, this Georgia Historical Commission postcard shows the fort's appearance from 1965 to 1975. On the very left side of the photograph, two mines (one painted black and one off-white) sit unobtrusively next to four stairs leading from the parade ground to the museum. A CHS staff member noted on the back of this postcard, "The mine on the left turned out to still be loaded with 300 lbs of TNT!" His note does not reveal the final fate of the mine. Below is the fort as it looked in November 1973. The state installed a cannon facing the river in front of the sally port.

Turnbull's Tavern was located 300 yards upriver from Fort Jackson. Nichol Turnbull, who sold the land to the government to build Fort Jackson, located his tavern here for many of the same reasons Fort Jackson is located at Five Fathom Hole; it is a natural stopping point and harbor for ships with thirsty sailors. The tavern appears on an 1825 map but was likely there earlier. Most of the artifacts found during an early-1970s reconnaissance survey were from the late 18th century. Examples include a 1738 Spanish coin cut in half, a 1775 silver coin, and a United States 1805 1¢ coin, which looked almost new. Clay tobacco pipes, bottle fragments, and buttons from the Revolutionary War to the Civil War were also found as well as structural remains seen in these photographs. The foundation corners, seen here, were unusual, made of both small handmade brick and ballast stone. These were very similar to other foundations the survey archaeologist observed in an early dig at the Davenport House in Savannah.

Talley Kirkland, who authored the survey report, advocated for the site to be preserved. Turnbull's Tavern was a famous tavern and was mostly undisturbed at the time of his report. However, he noted that the site, like all sites along the Savannah River, was in danger from erosion and dredging. At low tide, wooden wharf remains, the large hand-hewn timbers seen here, were visible in addition to stone foundations and artifacts scattered on the surface. Staff and locals who kept an eye on the site still reported artifacts in abundance as late as 2011, prior to Hurricanes Matthew and Irma in 2016 and 2017, respectively. However, in 2018, a subsequent site visit showed significantly fewer artifacts. The author's reconnaissance in 2020 found very few structural remains or artifacts. Beyond the riprap placed to anchor Fort Jackson's shoreline, the riverbank has been severely cut back and sharply drops four to five feet. Access to the site is very difficult, as the few archaeological remains are now along the soft riverbed, which is only exposed at the lowest tides.

In 1975, a tide gate was installed on the Savannah River. The goal was to increase the river's tidal flow, pushing more silt out of the river, therefore making dredging projects less frequent. The project was successful in this goal; however, the tides' increased forces caused more shoreline erosion and other environmental problems, negatively affecting the fort. The river bottom eroded so much that the timber pilings that formed the fort's foundation were visible, exposing them to corrosive elements. The fort was undercut so much that river water flowed under the moat wall, rather than through the tide tunnel. Without support, the tide tunnel began to "droop" six to eight inches, causing structural damage. The Army Corps of Engineers oversees the Savannah River harbor and, therefore, is responsible for negative impacts to historic properties caused by its harbor duties.

From 1977 to 1979, an extensive project was carried out to fix the fort's tide tunnel. The tide tunnel was raised to its original height, and a new deck with steel supports was created under the floor. A sheet piling wall was installed on all three sides about five feet from the tunnel walls and driven nearly 45 feet into the soil, leaving six inches above the surface. A concrete "deck" was created from the outer walls to the piling wall. The repairs took approximately a year, costing over $340,000. The tide tunnel needed a second round of repairs in 2007. First, archaeology was conducted on the tide tunnel's soil surface in the hopes of finding intact soil from the fort's construction. Unfortunately, due to the previous repairs, only modern artifacts (also known as trash) were found.

While the riprap securing the riverbank is still holding after nearly 50 years, the fort continues to flood with increasing regularity due to the human-caused climate crisis. There are two primary reasons the fort floods. Rising sea levels mean the river also is higher. Fort Jackson is about 13 miles upriver from the Atlantic Ocean, and the river has powerful tides, which can rise and fall between seven and ten feet every six hours. The second cause is increasingly powerful and frequent storms. Each time the fort floods, incremental damage is done. During high tides from November 12 to 14, 1981, the fort flooded and saltwater damaged the electrical system beyond repair. The Coastal Heritage Society had to replace the system, an expense that the fledgling nonprofit could ill afford.

Other disasters are directly man-made. On July 25, 1981, a freighter coming up the Savannah River lost power. The crew tried to drop both anchors but only one deployed, pulling the ship into Fort Jackson, horn sounding as she made impact. The British-registered, 593-foot bulk freighter *Practician* was not damaged. The fort, however, was severely damaged. The 12 pilings holding the floating dock were lost, and the stationary dock was smashed. Another part of the dock broke free and was later recovered, but it was an entire loss. This recently built dock was critical because boat tours used it to bring 10,000 visitors per year to the fort, one quarter of the entire visitation. These visitors came for dinner programs and were an essential source of funding in the Coastal Heritage Society's (CHS) early years, bringing in $5,000 per night.

The CHS newsletter used humorous headlines such as "British Ship Attacks Fort" to explain the seriousness of the problem. The *Practician*'s bulbous bow damaged the original cypress timber substructure and foundation. The damage was a one-two punch, as the fort needed money for repairs and was actively losing money without its dock. Fortunately, Joe Tanner, the Department of Natural Resources commissioner at the time, saw the incident on the news, had the boat arrested in the port, and successfully sued for damages. Had the ship not been arrested, it would have left port the next day without repercussions. The CHS would not have been able to repair the fort, and quite possibly the fort would have once again closed down. Repair work started well before the court case was settled because the CHS and the state were anxious to avoid further damage from neglect.

Improbably, the next month, another ship hit the fort in the same spot. Tugboats lost control of the *Cavala*, also a freighter. Fortunately, because the ship hit the same spot, no additional damage was done to the fort. Above, the remains of the crumpled dock are still visible and have not even been cleared yet. Over the course of more than two years, a new dock was built upstream and a 30- to 40-foot section of the fort's foundation was repaired at the cost of $285,000. At left, this picture is a bit of a mystery but is believed to show men working to repair the moat retaining wall in August 1983.

The Coastal Heritage Society has taken on historic preservation projects that did not immediately relate to Fort Jackson. Norfolk Southern Corporation donated the old Tybee Train Passenger Depot from a train line that ran from Savannah to Tybee Beach. Near the end of 1988, a barge moved the Tybee Passenger Depot down the Savannah River, then cranes were used to move it to land. With the help of many donations, the CHS rehabilitated the structure over the course of about two years. Since then, the depot has operated as the fort's orientation center and gift shop. Today, visitors exit a back door (left window in the picture at right) and down the path being laid here.

Natural elements like wind, rain, and the tides wear at the bricks over time. Increased boat traffic and deepening the harbor has resulted in more damage as waves lash at the fort. The mortar between bricks wears away faster than the bricks. Repointing brick is the process of scraping out old, decayed mortar and replacing it with fresh mortar. A critical part of the process is replicating the historic mortar properly. Preservationists need to think of the fort almost as a living organism that "breathes." The fort expands and contracts in the heat and cold, wet and dry. The bricks and mortar must work together in this movement, otherwise the bricks and mortar will pull apart, causing more problems. In 2000, the CHS received a Georgia Heritage Historic Preservation Grant to clean off vegetation (above) and repair the masonry (left).

The CHS received a prestigious Save America's Treasures grant for $300,000 in 2008 to do extensive maintenance and repairs. The first step was removal of vegetation that had grown into the structure (above). This process was aided with hand tools and even herbicides to retard future growth. Below, three stages are clear. To the left of the ladder, the brick has not been cleaned. To the right of the ladder, sections of new bright white mortar are obvious, while staff works on lower levels to repoint more cleaned brick. This picture was taken at low tide. Preservationists had to carefully time their work as the tide went out, giving them a few hours to work and some time for the mortar to set before the tide rose nearly to the top of the moat wall.

In November 2010, the Coastal Heritage Society archaeologists dug into the terreplein, or gun platform. The project was in advance of waterproofing the terreplein floor to prevent water from seeping down, collecting in the casemates below, and damaging the masonry as it trickled down. The archaeologists were looking for a historic drainage system, evidence of the fort's construction and use, and information about the soldiers' daily lives. Here, the author screens soil looking for artifacts. Archaeologists found few nonarchitectural artifacts, indicating soldiers probably spent little time on the terreplein, but the archaeologists did find several layers relating to how the terreplein was transformed over time. While the artifacts varied in age, the soil layers all dated to the late 1800s, showing that the soil was disturbed during the guns' final removal. Fortunately, several layers of floors lie below the soil.

The deepest, oldest floor layer was linear brick courses from the earliest casemates, which had flat roofs. In 1846, the casemates were redesigned with arched roofs, and granite foundations for gun traverses were added. Natural cement was laid across the casemate roof. Here, one granite traverse rail, which held a metal track allowing the cannon to swing left and right, is present (background), and one is missing (foreground). See the previous picture for an example of the metal track laid directly on the concrete floor. The closer traverse rail was likely removed during the early-1870s improvements to accommodate heavier 15-inch guns. Around 1896–1897, the guns were removed, and by the turn of the 20th century, there is no evidence of activity, just soil and overgrowth. The area was capped by a layer of yellow sand spread in 1966 as a foundation for the four-inch concrete slab currently in place. Archaeologists and the fort staff were extremely pleased with the great quantity of intact structures but failed in their goal to find any historic drainage features.

A month later, the CHS archaeologists completed a similar project on the c. 1873 shell magazine. Built during the fort's last renovation, this shell magazine held prepared shells filled with gunpowder. These had to be kept separate from the bulk gunpowder, held in the powder magazine next to the sally port. Historic preservationists were concerned about extreme moisture problems in the magazine and the casemates below the magazine. Archaeologists excavated into the sod roof to determine the roof's shape and see if there were artifacts that could speak to life at the fort. Not surprisingly, very few artifacts were found. The fort's highest, most exposed point would not be a place soldiers spent much time, therefore, they would not lose many artifacts there. Archaeologists were able to quickly clear the area and allow the building preservationists to proceed.

While there was not much found archaeologically, this project was fun logistically and involved lots of climbing, balancing, and creativity because the usual equipment would not sit on top of the rounded roof. Getting the soil from the top of the roof into a screen to check for artifacts was a major undertaking. The first set-up involved throwing the soil from the roof to the deck below and hoping to hit the screen. The redesign is shown here. The screen was placed on scaffolding, dirt was shovel-thrown into the screen until full (right), and then the archaeologist who was screening climbed out to check for artifacts (below).

Historic preservationists removed all of the soil from the basin-shaped concrete roof and repaired the cracks (above). Then they applied soil cloth, new soil, and resodded the roof (below). Sod roofs and earthworks are highly functional for fortifications. While stone and brick feels impressive to people, it cracks easily when hit with cannonballs and other projectiles. Sod and soil absorb the incoming ordnance with little damage to the overall structure. These were the original "green roofs," whose benefits are now being explored for many environmental reasons—they are cooler, produce oxygen, capture carbon, and reduce storm water runoff.

Six

Programming

Telling the Fort's Story

While Fort Jackson was a maritime museum, there was little active programming beyond guests viewing the exhibits. A Georgia Historical Commission staff member was present to answer questions. Once the Coastal Heritage Society (CHS) began operating and interpreting the fort on Labor Day in 1976, this changed dramatically. The natural consequence of this shift was frequently having staff and volunteers in period clothing showing the public what everyday life was like for the fort's soldiers. This included everything from firing muskets and cannons to cooking and craft demonstrations to building boats and structures. While the fort was active, buildings lined the walls. These buildings included several barracks, a kitchen, and privies, all of which were eventually dismantled. Over time, the CHS has added buildings for interpretation and programs, including pavilions where barracks once stood and smaller structures for craft interpretation such as the blacksmith shops. Fort Jackson also hosts special events such as weddings and dinners. These events support the fort as fundraisers and allow visitors the chance to experience the fort at special times, such as sunset. What follows is only a small sample of the volunteers and staff who have contributed to bringing the fort to life.

One exhibit holdover from the Georgia Historical Commission era was the periscope, seen here through the sally port with Eluigi Perkins doing masonry work to the left. This exhibit was neat in theory but in reality did not work very well. The viewing screen was often dirty and difficult to clean. Below is a view through the periscope looking upstream toward Savannah. The fort's walls can be seen at the very bottom. In June 1979, CHS got a grant to move the periscope to a more suitable location. Today, the periscope can be seen at Fort Screven, which is part of the Tybee Light Station and Museum.

The periscope can also be seen in this February 1978 picture of the fort. The Georgia Historical Commission installed the cannon in front of the sally port but not the guard shack to the right. Cannons are a crowd favorite, and cannon firings have always been a focus of fort programming.

This is a rare picture showing the inside of the state maritime museum extension in November 1973. From left to right are a binnacle from a Liberty ship, the name board from the SS *Casimir Pulaski* built at Southeastern Shipyard, and a wooden dugout canoe. The exhibits were through the open doors of the casemates to the right.

While the brick fort dates to 1808, a "mud fort," or earthen battery, was on-site during the Revolutionary War. When the Coastal Heritage Society first managed Fort Jackson, it commonly interpreted this era. These photographs are from a Revolutionary War camp in the winter of 1977–1978. With few exceptions, these reenactors were volunteers who brought their own period clothing, weapons, and other supplies. At left, two men portray 2nd South Carolina Continentals, who were professional American soldiers. Below, four men (a sergeant, a private, and two grenadiers in bearskin caps) reenact as British redcoats from the 60th Regiment of Foote. This regiment defended the Spring Hill Redoubt during the 1779 Battle of Savannah. The Coastal Heritage Society has expanded its Revolutionary War interpretation to downtown Savannah's Battlefield Memorial Park, the location of the 1779 Battle of Savannah.

These photographs show reenactors from another late-1970s Revolutionary War encampment. At right is a "camp follower," a fusilier (regular soldier) from the French Regiment du Foix, and a 2nd South Carolina Continental soldier. Below from left to right, two members of the French Regiment du Foix flank a free black soldier in the French Volunteers du Saint Domingue, a 2nd South Carolina Continental soldier, and a militiaman (part-time citizen-soldier) fire their muskets. The French and Haitian volunteers fought in the 1779 Battle of Savannah as American allies. The Haitian volunteers prevented the British from pursuing the retreating Allied forces.

It is known from the archaeology conducted in the 1960s that women and children were sometimes present at the fort. Women and children visiting or living at the fort were likely to be wives and children of the officers, who had more privileges. Women, often called "camp followers," were also employed as laundresses, cooks, and mess hall waitresses. The woman pictured here is cooking a stew or soup, and there are carrots on the bench in front of her. Volunteers like these would actually camp out at the fort, sleeping in their tents at night and cooking their meals over open fires using historically accurate techniques and foods. This added to the realism for visitors and allowed the reenactors to show more of 18th-century life, including wrinkled clothing and sore backs from sleeping on the ground. This also added to the fun for volunteers, who got to spend their entire weekend at the fort, seeing the fort from a perspective few get to see, including sunrises and sunsets. Hijinks often ensued.

Barba Negra, built in 1896 as the two-masted Norwegian whaling vessel *Moder*, has had many adventures, from harpooning whales to whale conservation and from racing to staying docked as a museum. In the 1970s, Albert Seidl and Gerhard Schwisow restored the ship, renaming her *Barba Negra* (translated as "Black Beard"). At New York City's Bicentennial Tall Ship Parade, the crew met Savannah mayor John Rousakis, which led to the ship's docking at Rousakis Plaza on River Street for 25 years. Tourists and locals would visit the ship and learn about shipboard life. The ship was also used for filming television shows and movies, and she occasionally visited Fort Jackson to participate in larger historical reenactments, as seen in the picture below.

As Fort Jackson saw more action during the Civil War, reenactors have also interpreted this war. The Confederates held Fort Jackson until December 20, 1864, evacuating the night before Union general William T. Sherman arrived and the Union army garrisoned Fort Jackson once again. Therefore, the fort has always interpreted both sides. Above, soldiers drill outside the fort while trying to stay warm. At left, Union soldiers prepare to enter the fort during a winter of 1977–1978 reenactor encampment. Union troops that garrisoned Fort Jackson include the 137th New York Infantry Regiment, the 29th Ohio Infantry Regiment, the 28th Pennsylvania Infantry Regiment, and the 55th Massachusetts Infantry Regiment.

Like the Revolutionary War encampments, volunteers set up tents and really lived at the fort for the weekend. The men and women would reenact life at the fort, including daily chores of equipment maintenance, cooking, and drilling with their muskets. The soldiers would take turns guarding the sally port, which despite the sun was a very cold job in the winter. Historians and archaeologists also use reenacting to learn more about life in the past by actually trying it on. Researchers gather data to answer questions such as how well did this equipment work? How miserable is it sleeping in a Civil War tent in February? And how easy is it to break a tooth on hardtack?

Often volunteers would form groups to reenact a specific military unit. These men represent the 1st New York Engineers at an encampment in 1977. These groups would often volunteer together for years. In September 1981, the 1st New York Engineers, who were based in the Jacksonville, Florida, area, helped construct a boat shed at Fort Jackson. The group also helped to construct the first pavilion and a temporary building to hold the Smith & Porter steam engine when it first arrived at Fort Jackson. The workers used period-appropriate tools, interpreting building skills as well as military skills to the public. During the Civil War, the 1st New York Engineers were involved in the siege and capture of Fort Pulaski, then mostly operated in South Carolina and Virginia but were never stationed at Fort Jackson.

The 22nd Georgia Heavy Artillery Battalion, Company A (Bartow Artillery) and Company B (Wise Guards) were stationed at Fort Jackson for nearly two years. Company A was one of the last to evacuate. These photographs date to November 1978. In April 1979, the new 22nd Georgia Heavy Artillery Battalion, Company A, Bartow Artillery was declared the fort's first official reenacting garrison. The group remained very active in volunteering at Fort Jackson for many years. Above, the group, which included women, is socializing. Below, the company demonstrates a cannon firing. Note the two individuals sitting on the fort's parapet.

Fort Jackson staff and volunteers demonstrated many crafts and professions over the years. Blacksmithing is always popular and dramatic. John Roberson, wearing suspenders in both pictures, was a master blacksmith who used his skills over nearly four decades at Fort Jackson to teach visitors and school groups. He also made repairs and crafted new iron pieces for everything from rehabilitating the Smith & Porter steam engine to building new cannon carriages. Roberson also used his skills to teach others to blacksmith and fabricate exhibits for other Coastal Heritage Society–managed properties such as the Savannah History Museum and the Georgia State Railroad Museum.

The first annual Scottish Games were held at Fort Jackson on May 6, 1978. The Scottish Games are an annual festival celebrating Scottish culture in Savannah. Traditional live music with bagpipers and drummers performing have always been part of the celebration. Old Fort Jackson hosted the games into the 2000s.

Highland dancers in colorful traditional dress also performed. Highland dance is a rigorous activity needing strength, athleticism, and grace. These young women are dancing to live music courtesy of the single bagpiper behind the stage. Today, young people compete in the Highland Dancing Southern Regional Championships at the Scottish Games.

Athletic competitions are also extremely popular. Pictured is the caber toss, where competitors throw a large caber, or pole, so the caber spins end over end away from the tosser. The tosser is scored based on how much the caber rotates and whether the caber falls away from (good) or toward (bad) the tosser. Today, athletes also compete in the sheaf toss, Scottish hammer throw, and open stone put. Other activities at the games include activities for kids, sheepherding, reenactments, clan booths, and vendors with food and other items. The 2020 games were canceled due to the COVID-19 pandemic.

An early and vital Coastal Heritage Society fundraising method was dinners at the fort. These dinners were especially popular with groups from the Savannah Convention Center. Capt. Sam Stevens was also an early supporter, bringing his Harbor Queen Riverboat Company tours to the fort for programming and dinners. Dinners usually featured local foods (before it was cool) such as oyster roasts and Lowcountry boil. At one point, Fort Jackson boasted the largest wood-fired oyster cooker on the East Coast. Local restaurant Johnny Harris, which began as a barbecue pit and speakeasy on Victory Drive in 1924, sometimes catered the dinners.

Visitors would disembark at the dock for dinner and a historical program led by interpreters in period clothing. These evening programs often featured historical narratives and musket demonstrations as well as the always popular cannon firings. Visitors were able to roam around the fort and watch the sun set. Being at a historic site after hours is always a bit of a thrill for history nerds. Due to its proximity to the river and low, marshy location, mosquitoes and no-see-ums (or biting sand gnats) are a constant problem, especially when the weather is at its most pleasant. Many cans of bug spray were always a critical ingredient in Fort Jackson dinners.

In 1898, a Shetland Island local built the *Venus* with driftwood using generations-old techniques not dissimilar to ones used on Viking long ships. The *Venus* was a traditional fishing vessel for decades. Paul Earling Johnstone bought the *Venus* in 1964 and made her into a small yacht by adding a deck, cabin, and Bermuda yawl rig. Johnstone did long distance sailing, even crossing the Atlantic Ocean in 1965. Shortly after this, the boat landed in storage at Fort Jackson. In 1982, the boat was transported back to Scotland on the MV *Troll Viking* to the West of Scotland Boat Museum in Glasgow, which is today the Scottish Maritime Museum.

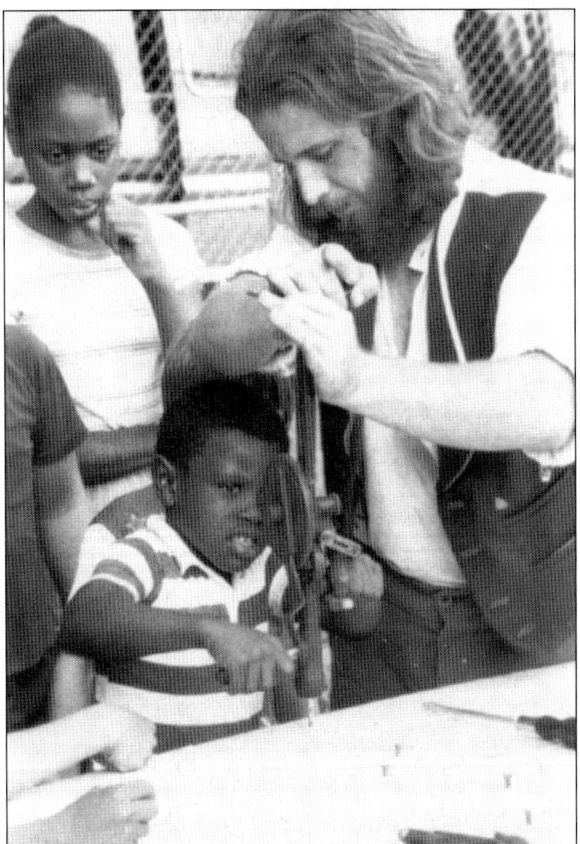

Program specialist John Merret teaches children about traditional crafts in a July 22, 1982, Maritime Heritage Program. Above, Merret wears period-appropriate clothing and demonstrates knot tying, a critical skill for sailing as the children show varying levels of understanding and skepticism in his lesson. At left, children test out a hand-powered drill. As the Coastal Heritage Society expanded its programming, children's activities and school field trips became a focus that continues to today. Hands-on programming like these activities are often the best way to engage the public, especially children, who love to be active and often do not realize they are learning something while they play.

During the Labor Day program in 1982, a boy attempts to make bricks. Most of Fort Jackson's bricks are Savannah grey bricks, likely produced at the Hermitage Plantation, and handmade roughly the same way that is being practiced here. Clay is mixed and kneaded with any necessary inclusions such as sand and pushed into molds. The unmolded bricks air dry, then are fired in kilns. Before the Civil War, enslaved people made these bricks. After 1865, African Americans were employed to turn out huge numbers of bricks, producing a relatively cheap but quality building product and making the plantation owners extremely wealthy.

The Coastal Heritage Society traditionally salutes all military ships that pass Fort Jackson with a cannon firing. Other ships are saluted on request, or if CHS wishes to honor a particular ship. Above, a staff member is about to fire a cannon while a US Navy cargo ship passes. This ship is an Algol-class vehicle cargo ship (also known as fast sealift ships) and is the fastest type of cargo ship in the world. All ships of this class are owned by the US Navy, and all are named after bright stars. Below, the cannon has just fired as a US Coast Guard ship passes.

In September 1993, the CHS and Beach High School JROTC students officially formed the 1st Regiment South Carolina Infantry, Company A, volunteer reenactment unit. The previous summer, Fort Jackson hosted a weekend encampment for 15 participants of the 1st South Carolina with two members of the 54th Massachusetts as instructors. The original unit was the first African American regiment in the US Army, formed in May 1862 and mustered in January 31, 1863, in Beaufort, South Carolina. Formerly enslaved on plantations in Georgia, South Carolina, and Florida, the soldiers operated mostly in the South Carolina Lowcountry and coastal areas near Jacksonville, Florida. The unit was reorganized into the 33rd Regiment, United States Colored Infantry in early 1864. The 33rd was in Savannah from March 8 to June 6, 1865. Seventeen soldiers from this unit won the Congressional Medal of Honor.

Above, actor Cary Elwes, center, speaks to CHS director Scott Smith, right, and a crew member during filming of the movie *Glory*. The movie, which premiered in early 1990, tells the story of the 54th Massachusetts Infantry Regiment, which did spend time briefly in Savannah. The 55th Massachusetts Infantry Regiment, essentially an overflow from the 54th, was stationed at Forts Jackson, Lee, and Bartow in 1865. The movie, starring Matthew Broderick, Denzel Washington, Morgan Freeman, and Andre Braugher, won many awards, including three Oscars, a Golden Globe, a Grammy, and an NAACP Image Award. Below, extras receive instructions before filming.

At right, the HMS *Rose* sails to Fort Jackson for a field trip fair in June 1991. The original British ship was built around 1757 and scuttled in Savannah in 1779. This replica was built in 1970 and modified for use in filming two movies. Below, cannon firings are a perennial favorite with fort guests, especially at night. At right in this photograph, a man wears a gray Confederate military kepi (French military cap) and vest with sky blue trousers, possibly representing the Republican Blues, who were stationed at Fort Jackson during the Civil War. At left, John Roberson stands at attention in his CSS *Georgia* sailor uniform.